Independent
Reading Management Kit:
Genre

by Laura Witmer

■SCHOLASTIC
Teaching
Resources

New York ◆ Toronto ◆ London ◆ Auckland ◆ Sydney
Mexico City ◆ New Delhi ◆ Hong Kong ◆ Buenos Aires

To my family and friends—
thanks for your support and encouragement.

Cover and interior design by Gerard Fuchs
Cover and interior illustration by Mike Moran

ISBN: 0-439-44514-0
Copyright © 2003 by Laura Witmer
All rights reserved. Published by Scholastic Inc.
Printed in the U.S.A.

2 3 4 5 6 7 8 9 10   40   09 08 07 06 05 04 03

Table of Contents

Introduction

The purpose of this book is to provide teachers with a way to help students become independent and responsible readers. In my ten years of teaching, I have discovered that many teachers, including myself, spend too much time concentrating only on reading skills and not enough time simply letting students read. We need to allow our students to be more responsible for their own reading, as well as provide our struggling readers with adequate practice. Reading is like any of the other subjects we teach: students need to practice in order to succeed.

This book describes the program I developed to help students become more successful independent readers. I found that even the most reluctant readers enjoy working through an interesting literature project. Literature projects also provide a way for me to keep track of the progress my students are making while reading independently. Giving students a choice in their projects allows them to take responsibility for their own reading progress. It also allows each student to work at his or her own pace and interest level. I have used this program with all types of students. Students with reading disabilities are able to participate and work at a level where they feel confident. Even my most challenged readers start to feel good about themselves and their reading progress.

How to Use This Book

The activities in this book may be used as an independent reading program, or they can be used to supplement your existing reading program. The book covers the nine main genres. For each genre, there is a tic-tac-toe title page that lists the nine projects available for students to complete.

Teacher Tip

Organizing Your Classroom Library
To help students choose books from the appropriate genre, I put books from a specific genre together on one shelf. I then use stick-on labels to identify which shelf holds which genre. Gathering books is the hardest part. I have found books at library sales, garage sales, and secondhand bookstores, and have purchased books through book clubs. Students can also go to the library to find a book.

Organizing Your Forms

In order to simplify running your independent reading program, make multiple copies of all the activity sheets. I store my project sheets in colored hanging folders in a plastic crate. I use a different color folder for each genre. For example, yellow folders are for historical fiction. Label each hanging folder with the genre and the project name. Students can then be responsible for finding needed forms on their own.

Introducing the Process

There are several steps I use to introduce the independent reading projects to my students. At the beginning of each new genre, I copy the title tic-tac-toe page and all the project instruction pages. (I cut apart the pages that have two projects on them.) When I give my students the project packet, I go through each project to explain the requirements. I explain that they are to choose their projects in a tic-tac-toe pattern. I then give my students a chance to choose a book that meets the genre requirements. Once the book is chosen, I give them a due date for their projects. They record the due date on their tic-tac-toe page. I give them at least a month to read their book and complete the projects.

Teacher Tip

Materials
Almost all the projects require paper and pencils or pens. Only additional materials, beyond paper and pen, are listed for each project. You should have a supply of both lined and unlined paper available for your students.

Assessing Student Work

Each project has its own rubric designed specifically for that project. After students have decided what genre projects they will complete, I make a copy of the grading summary page for that genre. For each student, put a check in the box next to the three projects he or she plans to complete. I grade the projects as students complete them. When they've completed all three, I record the final total on the summary line at the bottom. This is their final grade. I sometimes allow them to pick a fourth project to use for extra credit.

Displaying Student Work

Once the projects are turned in for final grading, I choose some exemplary work to display around the room. I like for students to see what the other projects look like. It is also motivating to students who may be moving to a new genre to see what projects they will soon be working on.

Individualized Reading Contract

Name _____ Date _____

Book Title _____

Genre _____ Author _____

Reading Plan

I plan to read from page _____ to page _____ by _____.
(date)

I plan to read from page _____ to page _____ by _____.
(date)

I plan to read from page _____ to page _____ by _____.
(date)

I plan to read from page _____ to page _____ by _____.
(date)

I plan to read from page _____ to page _____ by _____.
(date)

I plan to read from page _____ to page _____ by _____.
(date)

List the three tic-tac-toe activities you plan to do for your book.

1. _____

2. _____

3. _____

Independent Reading Management Kit: Genre Scholastic Teaching Resources

Historical Fiction Projects

Name _____ Due Date _____

Book Title:_____

✦ Make a tic-tac-toe by choosing three projects to complete for your novel.

Vocabulary Cards	**Event Map**	**Character Prediction**
Character Comparison	**Design a Package**	**Change the Setting**
Select a Quote	**Rewrite a Boring Part**	**Story Chain**

— Historical Fiction

Vocabulary Cards

What you'll need:

ten index cards

Steps:

❶ Choose ten vocabulary words from your book. Write each word on the first line on the lined side of the card.

❷ Next, write a definition of the word using clues from the text.

❸ Then, write the dictionary definition.

❹ On the blank side of the card, tell how the definitions are alike and how they are different.

Grading Criteria	
Chose ten words	10 points
Dictionary definitions	10 points
Text clue definitions	10 points
Followed directions	10 points
Mechanics	5 points
Neatness	5 points
	50 points

Event Map

What you'll need:

Event Map sheet (page 13)

Steps:

❶ Choose the most significant event in your book.

❷ Follow the directions on the Event Map to tell about the event.

Grading Criteria	
Event map explanations	20 points
Followed directions	20 points
Mechanics	5 points
Neatness	5 points
	50 points

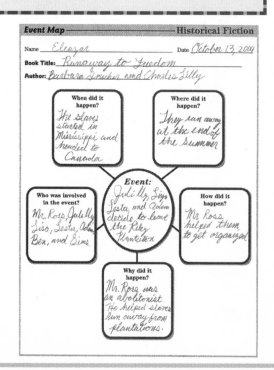

Character Prediction

Steps:

After you have finished reading your book, predict what will happen next to an important character by writing a new ending to the story. Briefly summarize the ending of the book (in about one paragraph).

Eleazar

Island of the Blue Dolphins

Karana goes to the live at the mission, but she's very unhappy. She feels so different from everyone there. She never feels like she fits in. She misses all the animals she had made friends with. Most importantly, she misses her independence. Eventually, she decides to leave the mission to try to return to her island. She has decided that being independent is more important than being around people.

Grading Criteria

Summary of story ending	15 points
New ending	20 points
Followed directions	5 points
Mechanics	5 points
Neatness	5 points
	50 points

Character Comparison

What you'll need:

Character Comparison sheet (page 14)

Grading Criteria

Same qualities	20 points
Different qualities	20 points
Followed directions	5 points
Neatness	5 points
	50 points

Steps:

❶ Choose a character from your story.

❷ Complete the Character Comparison sheet. List ways you are the same as the character you chose, and then list ways you are different

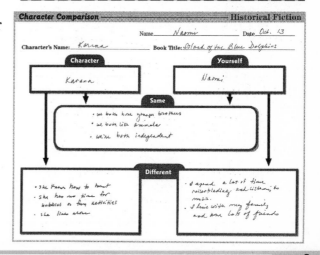

Design a Package

What you'll need:

empty cereal box, white paper to cover cereal box, colored pencils or markers, tape

Steps:

❶ Cover the cereal box completely with white paper.

❷ Create a packaging design for a food product that you read about in your book. Be sure the design fits with the time period of your book.

❸ Be sure to include a catchy name for your product.

Grading Criteria

Ad accurately depicts time period of the novel	15 points
Graphics	10 points
Cereal box layout	10 points
Creativity	10 points
Neatness/colorfulness of box	5 points
	50 points

Change the Setting

Steps:

❶ Briefly describe the current setting of the story.

❷ Think of a new setting for the story and describe it in a paragraph.

❸ Tell how the story and its characters would be affected if the setting and time period were changed.

Grading Criteria

Summary of current setting	15 points
Description of the new setting	15 points
Explanation of setting effects	10 points
Mechanics	5 points
Neatness	5 points
	50 points

Kailah

Runaway to Freedom takes place on a plantation in the 1870s.

I would like to change the setting to a ranch in Montana in 1950.

The novel would be completely different if the setting and time were changed. The novel is about how four slaves run away from their plantation to find freedom in Canada. If the setting were changed to a Montana ranch, the plot of the story wouldn't work because the slaves would not have to leave their home and travel to another country just to live freely. The characters' lives would be better if the setting were changed. They could own property and live together as a family. I think the ranch setting would fit Julilly better because she dreamed about being free and not having to work for mean men that whip her if she doesn't work fast enough.

Historical Fiction

Select a Quote

Steps:

❶ Skim through your book and select a short quote that made you pause and think.

❷ Write the title and author of the book on a sheet of paper.

❸ Copy the quote and page number.

❹ Explain why this quote appealed to you. How did it make you feel? What did it make you think or visualize?

❺ Show how the quote connects to a theme, event, or character in the book.

❻ Then tell how the quote connects to your life or to another book.

Grading Criteria

Quote from the novel	5 points
Explanation	20 points
Quotation connections	20 points
Neatness	5 points
	50 points

Rewrite a Boring Part

Steps:

❶ Skim through the book and choose a part of the book that you found boring.

❷ Summarize this part of the book.

❸ Rewrite this part to make it more exciting. Add details that would help to make it more interesting. Remember to keep the new part you write consistent with the story plot.

Grading Criteria

Summary of boring part	15 points
Adequate details in rewritten part	20 points
Followed directions	5 points
Mechanics	5 points
Neatness	5 points
	50 points

Story Chain

Historical Fiction

What you'll need:

ten sentence strips, pens or markers, tape

Steps:

1 On the first sentence strip, write the title and the author of the novel you read.

2 On the second sentence strip, tell where the story is taking place.

3 On the third sentence strip, tell who the characters are in the novel. Give a brief description of each character.

4 Choose seven important events in the story. Write one event on each of the seven remaining sentence strips. Make sure you include enough details about the event so that an outsider who hasn't read the book would understand the sequence of the story.

5 Use your sentence strips to make a linked chain. Make sure you tape them together in order.

Grading Criteria

Setting	5 points
Characters and descriptions	10 points
Important events	25 points
Followed directions	5 points
Neatness	5 points
	50 points

Name _____ Date _____

Book Title: _____

Author: _____

When did it
happen?

Where did it
happen?

Event:

Who was involved
in the event?

How did it
happen?

Why did it
happen?

Character Comparison ——— Historical Fiction

Book Title: _____

Name _____

Author: _____

Date _____

Character

Yourself

Same

Different

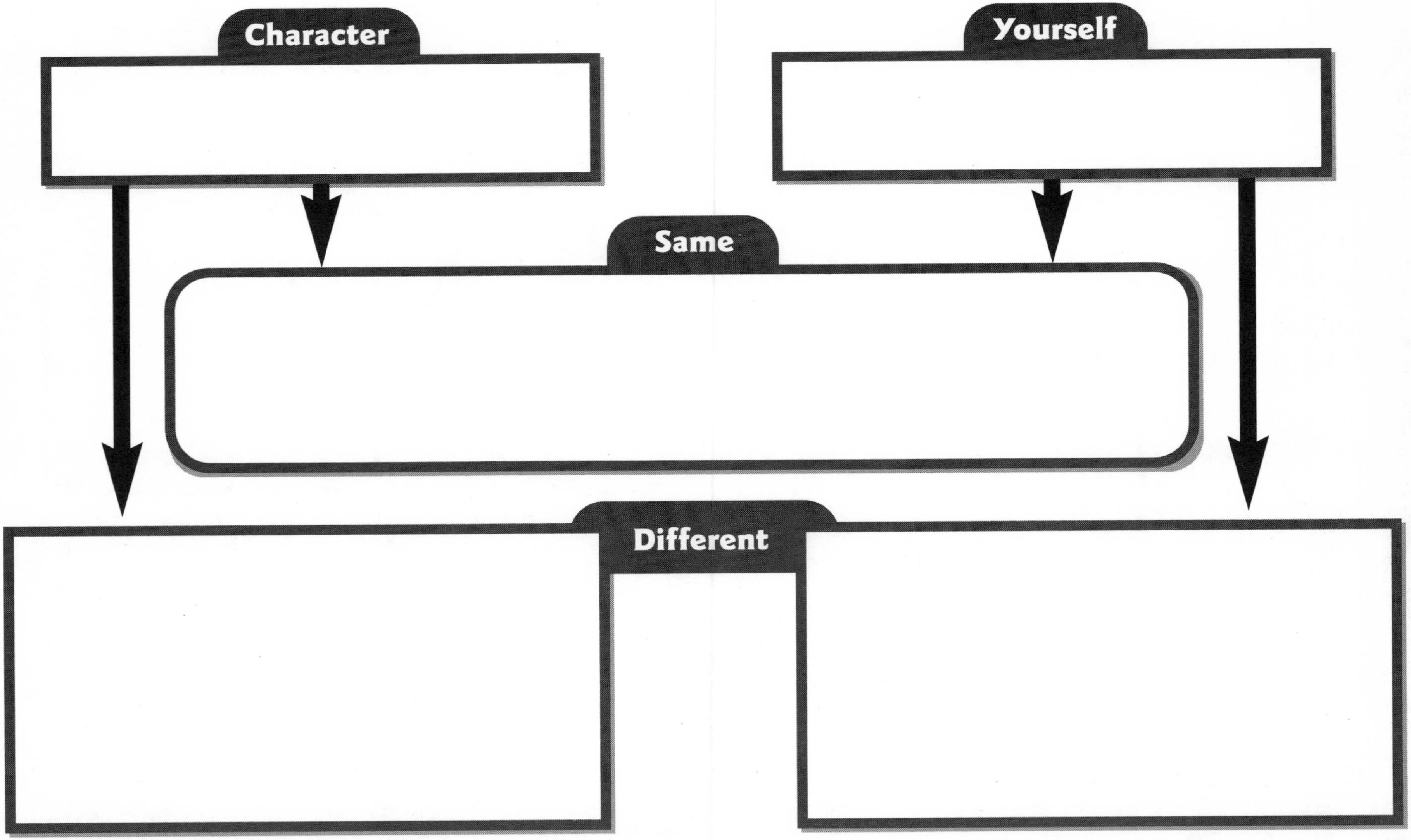

Grading Summary ———————— Historical Fiction

	Possible Score	My Score
❑ **Vocabulary Cards**		
Chose ten words	10 points	_____
Dictionary definitions	10 points	_____
Text clue definitions	10 points	_____
Followed directions	10 points	_____
Mechanics	5 points	_____
Neatness	5 points	_____
	50 points	_____
❑ **Event Map**		
Event map explanations	20 points	_____
Followed directions	20 points	_____
Mechanics	5 points	_____
Neatness	5 points	_____
	50 points	_____
❑ **Character Prediction**		
Summary of story ending	15 points	_____
New ending	20 points	_____
Followed directions	5 points	_____
Mechanics	5 points	_____
Neatness	5 points	_____
	50 points	_____
❑ **Character Comparison**		
Same qualities	20 points	_____
Different qualities	20 points	_____
Followed directions	5 points	_____
Neatness	5 points	_____
	50 points	_____
❑ **Design a Package**		
Ad accurately depicts time period of the novel	15 points	_____
Graphics	10 points	_____
Cereal box layout	10 points	_____
Creativity	10 points	_____
Neatness/colorfulness of box	5 points	_____
	50 points	_____

Grading Summary ———————— Historical Fiction

	Possible Score	My Score

❑ Change the Setting ....

Summary of current setting	.15 points	_____
Description of the new setting	.15 points	_____
Explanation of setting effects	.10 points	_____
Mechanics	. 5 points	_____
Neatness	. 5 points	_____
	50 points	_____

❑ Select a Quote ....

Quote from the novel	. 5 points	_____
Explanation	.20 points	_____
Quotation connections	.20 points	_____
Neatness	. 5 points	_____
	50 points	_____

❑ Rewrite a Boring Part ....

Summary of boring part	.15 points	_____
Adequate details in rewritten part	.20 points	_____
Followed directions	.5 points	_____
Mechanics	.5 points	_____
Neatness	. 5 points	_____
	50 points	_____

❑ Story Chain ....

Setting	.5 points	_____
Characters and descriptions	.10 points	_____
Important events	.25 points	_____
Followed directions	. 5 points	_____
Neatness	. 5 points	_____
	50 points	_____

Total for all three projects _____

Mystery Projects

Name _____ Due Date _____

Book Title:_____

✦ Make a tic-tac-toe by choosing three projects to complete for your novel.

Clue Journal	**Write a News Story**	**Story Map**
Problem Identification	**Emotion Time Line**	**Design a Game**
Pyramid Triorama	**Illustrate a Quote**	**Character Scrapbook**

Clue Journal

What you'll need:

small sheet of construction paper, colored pencils or markers, stapler

Grading Criteria

Organization	10 points
Adequate supporting details	10 points
Length requirement	10 points
Prediction	5 points
Followed directions	5 points
Mechanics	5 points
Neatness	5 points
	50 points

Steps:

❶ Create a clue journal for your mystery. Start by using the construction paper to design a cover for the journal. Be sure it includes the book's title and the author's name.

❷ On the first page, write a few sentences identifying the problem in the story.

❸ As you read your novel, record any clues that are introduced, one per page. Be sure to include the page number on which the clue appears.

❹ After you record a clue, tell whether you think it is important to the story and explain why.

❺ When you get to the second-to-last chapter, make a prediction about who you think committed the crime. Label this page "Final Prediction."

❻ On the last page of the journal, tell who committed the crime and whether your prediction was right or wrong.

❼ Staple the pages and cover together to form a book.

Write a News Story

What you'll need:

News Story sheet (page 24)

Grading Criteria

Organization	10 points
Followed directions	10 points
Adequate supporting details	10 points
Length requirement	10 points
Mechanics	5 points
Neatness	5 points
	50 points

Steps:

❶ Complete the News Story sheet for your mystery.

❷ Using the News Story sheet as your guideline, write a news story that summarizes the book. The summary should be at least three-quarters of a page typed or one and a half pages hand-written.

Story Map

Mystery

What you'll need:

Story Map sheet (page 25)

Steps:

❶ As you read your story, complete the Story Map sheet.

❷ If you need more room to record the problem solution steps, use the back of the sheet.

Grading Criteria

Setting identification	5 points
Problem identification	10 points
Solution identification	5 points
Solution steps	15 points
Followed directions	5 points
Mechanics	5 points
Neatness	5 points
	50 points

Problem Identification

What you'll need:

Problem Identification sheet (page 26)

Steps:

❶ Think of a problem that faced the character in your story. Write that problem in a complete sentence on the Problem Identification sheet.

❷ Identify three solutions that the character could have used to resolve the problem.

❸ Rank these solutions from 1 to 3, with 1 being the best, 3 being the worst.

❹ Explain your number 1 choice.

Grading Criteria

Problem identification	15 points
Solution identification	15 points
Reason	10 points
Followed directions	5 points
Neatness	5 points
	50 points

Problem Identification — **Mystery**

Name _Edgar_   Date _Jan. 11_

Character's Problem:

Claudia is determined to find out whether the statue in the Metropolitan Museum is really the work of Michelangelo.

3 Solutions: Rank from 1–3. On the back of this sheet, tell why you made your number 1 choice.

Rank

[2] They can do research at the library.

[1] They can visit Mrs. Frankweiler.

[3] They can drag the museum figures it out.

Emotion Time Line

What you'll need:

two sentence strips, Emotion Time Line sheet (page 27), Feeling Words Chart (page 28), tape, ruler, colored pencils or markers, index cards

Grading Criteria

Emotional statements	20 points
Explanations	20 points
Followed directions	5 points
Neatness	5 points
	50 points

Steps:

❶ Tape the two sentence strips together along the short ends to make a time line.

❷ Mark off three-inch sections along the time line. Start by measuring three inches from the left side of the time line, and continuing to the edge of the right side. Label each section with a chapeter number.

❸ As you read each chapter in your book, record the two feelings of the main character on the Emotion Time Line sheet. Use the Feeling Words Chart if you need help coming up with the right words to explain how the character felt.

❹ Choose one feeling. Holding the index cards vertically, write a description of how the character felt and why he or she had this feeling for each chapter on the time line.

❺ Tape the index cards onto the sentence strips below the appropriate chapter number.

❻ After you have finished reading the novel, choose one of the character's emotions that you have also experienced. Write the emotion on the back of the Emotion Time Line sheet and tell about when you felt this way.

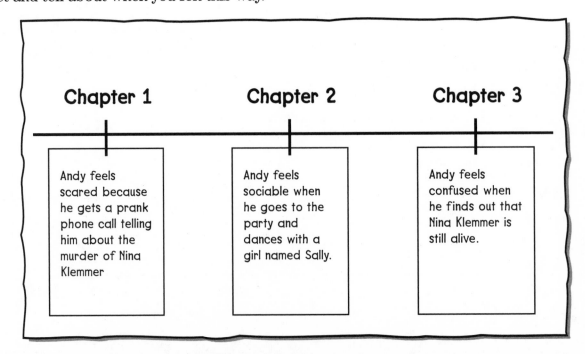

Chapter 1

Andy feels scared because he gets a prank phone call telling him about the murder of Nina Klemmer

Chapter 2

Andy feels sociable when he goes to the party and dances with a girl named Sally.

Chapter 3

Andy feels confused when he finds out that Nina Klemmer is still alive.

Design a Game

What you'll need:

file folder, colored pencils or markers

Grading Criteria

Well-designed game board	15 points
Question cards	10 points
Followed directions	10 points
Written directions	5 points
Colorful	5 points
Neatness	5 points
	50 points

Steps:

❶ Design a game based on the mystery novel you read. Use the file folder for the game board. (You may want to model your game on popular board games.)

❷ Your game should include cards with questions about your book. Players will need to answer the questions on the cards correctly in order to move their game pieces.

❸ Decorate your game board with images or symbols related to your book.

❹ Give your game a catchy title.

Pyramid Triorama

What you'll need:

four sheets of small white construction paper, scissors, tape, pencil, colored pencils or markers.

Steps:

❶ Fold the top left corner of a sheet of construction paper diagonally so that the top edge of the paper is flush with the right edge of the paper.

❷ Fold the top right corner diagonally so that it touches the lower point of the previous fold.

❸ Fold the rectangular panel at the bottom up. Cut off the panel.

❹ Open the paper up and cut the lower left diagonal crease up to the center point of the paper.

❺ Repeat steps 1–4 so you can create three more trioramas.

❻ For each triorama, fold one flap over the other and tape.

❼ Choose four important scenes from your mystery novel. Recreate the scenes in each of the trioramas.

❽ Tape the four trioramas together to make a pyramid.

❾ Explain each scene by writing a paragraph about it on lined paper.

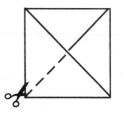

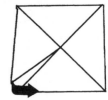

Grading Criteria	
Followed directions	10 points
Organization	15 points
Adequate details	15 points
Colorful	5 points
Neatness	5 points
	50 points

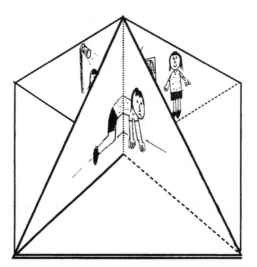

Illustrate a Quote

What you'll need:

colored pencils or markers

Steps:

❶ Choose a quote from your book that you feel is important, or that seems to speak to you.

❷ Write your chosen quote on the bottom of a sheet of unlined paper.

❸ Above the quote create an illustration to match your quote.

❹ On the back of the paper, tell why you chose this quote.

Grading Criteria

Quote from the novel	5 points
Explanation	20 points
Illustration	20 points
Neatness	5 points
	50 points

Character Scrapbook

What you'll need:

stapler, scissors, glue, magazines you can cut up, colored pencils or markers

Steps:

❶ Fold four sheets of plain paper together in half horizontally. Then staple them along the fold to make a book.

❷ On the front cover of your book, write the title: " _____ (the main character's name) Scrapbook." Decorate the cover to match the main character's style.

❸ Open to the first page and draw a portrait of the main character. Write the character's name.

❹ On the remaining pages, draw pictures or find pictures from magazines of items that relate to the character.

❺ Glue the pictures into the book or color the pictures you have drawn.

❻ Add captions to the pictures that tell how they relate to the character.

❼ Staple the pages and the cover together.

Grading Criteria

Organization	10 points
Adequate details	20 points
Reasoning for pictures	10 points
Followed directions	5 points
Neatness	5 points
	50 points

Name _____ Date _____

News Story Topic	News Story Headline

News Story Opening Sentence

Who is the story about? *List details*

When did the story happen? *List details*

What happened in the story? *List details*

Why did it happen? *List details*

Where did it happen? *List details*

Story Map ——————————————————— Mystery

Name _____ Date _____

Book Title: _____

Setting	Main Characters

Problem

Steps Taken to Solve Problem
(List as many as you need to retell the main action.)

Problem Solution

Problem Identification — Mystery

Name ______________________________ Date ______________

Character's Problem:

3 Solutions: Rank from 1 to 3. On the back of this sheet, tell why you made your number 1 choice.

Rank

☐ ______________________________

☐ ______________________________

☐ ______________________________

Name _____ Date _____

Chapter: ············

1.

2.

Chapter: ············

1.

2.

Chapter: ············

1.

2.

Chapter: ············

1.

2.

Chapter: ············

1.

2.

Chapter: ············

1.

2.

Chapter: ············

1.

2.

Chapter: ············

1.

2.

Chapter: ············

1.

2.

Chapter: ············

1.

2.

Feeling Words Chart ———————————— Mystery

Name _____ Date _____

scared	mad	relaxed	enraged
sleepy	disgusted	tied up in knots	timid
quiet	hungry	shaky	anxious
breathless	tired	nervous	delighted
weak	happy	overwhelmed	grim
afraid	friendly	excited	safe
triumphant	joyful	embarrassed	confused
confident	vulnerable	lonely	slow
serious	unhappy	cowardly	ugly
crazy	bothered	thrilled	sad
strong	paranoid	upset	glum
pleasant	sociable	reserved	shocked
gracious	content	cheerful	tense
pleased	miserable	angry	glad
gloomy	sorrowful	melancholic	bitter
discontent	chilly	helpless	calm
somber	solemn	peaceful	hurt
like a failure	abandoned	deserted	lost
pressured	defeated	lonesome	secure
certain	furious	positive	brave

Independent Reading Management Kit: Genre Scholastic Teaching Resources, page 28

Grading Summary ———————————————— Mystery

	Possible Score	**My Score**

❑ Clue Journal ....

	Possible Score	My Score
Organization	.10 points	_____
Adequate supporting details	.10 points	_____
Length requirement	.10 points	_____
Prediction	.5 points	_____
Followed directions	5 points	_____
Mechanics	5 points	_____
Neatness	5 points	_____
	50 points	_____

❑ Write a News Story ....

	Possible Score	My Score
Organization	.10 points	_____
Followed directions	.10 points	_____
Adequate supporting details	.10 points	_____
Length requirement	.10 points	_____
Mechanics	5 points	_____
Neatness	5 points	_____
	50 points	_____

❑ Story Map ....

	Possible Score	My Score
Setting identification	.5 points	_____
Problem identification	.10 points	_____
Solution identification	.5 points	_____
Solution Steps	.15 points	_____
Followed directions	.5 points	_____
Mechanics	.5 points	_____
Neatness	5 points	_____
	50 points	_____

❑ Problem Identification ....

	Possible Score	My Score
Problem identification	.15 points	_____
Solution identification	.15 points	_____
Reason	.10 points	_____
Followed directions	.5 points	_____
Neatness	5 points	_____
	50 points	_____

Grading Summary ——————————————— Mystery

	Possible Score	**My Score**

☐ Emotion Time Line ....

Emotional statements	.20 points	_____
Explanations	.20 points	_____
Followed directions	.5 points	_____
Neatness	. 5 points	_____
	50 points	_____

☐ Design a Game ....

Well-designed game board	.15 points	_____
Question cards	.10 points	_____
Followed directions	.10 points	_____
Written directions	.5 points	_____
Colorful	.5 points	_____
Neatness	. 5 points	_____
	50 points	_____

☐ Pyramid Triorama ....

Followed directions	.10 points	_____
Organization	.15 points	_____
Adequate details	.15 points	_____
Colorful	.5 points	_____
Neatness	. 5 points	_____
	50 points	_____

☐ Illustrate a Quote ....

Quote from the novel	.5 points	_____
Explanation	.20 points	_____
Illustration	.20 points	_____
Neatness	. 5 points	_____
	50 points	_____

☐ Character Scrapbook ....

Organization	.10 points	_____
Adequate details	.20 points	_____
Reasoning for pictures	.10 points	_____
Followed directions	.5 points	_____
Neatness	. 5 points	_____
	50 points	_____

Total for all three projects _____

Adventure Projects

Name _____ Due Date _____

Book Title: _____

✦ Make a tic-tac-toe by choosing three projects to complete for your novel.

Event Time Line	**Problem Chain**	**Novel News**
Story Map	**Character Journal Entries**	**Setting Map**
Adventure Brochure	**Conflict Chart**	**Life Connections**

Event Time Line

What you'll need:

eight 4-inch squares of paper, glue, two sheets of 9-by-18-inch white construction paper

Grading Criteria

Chronological order of events	15 points
Event explanation	10 points
Connections	10 points
Followed directions	5 points
Mechanics	5 points
Neatness	5 points
	50 points

Steps:

❶ As you read your book, record information about important events on the squares.

❷ Glue two pieces of construction paper together by the short ends.

❸ Glue the completed squares onto the construction paper in a pattern that shows the chronological order of the events.

❹ Choose two events that you can connect to your life, another book, or a world event.

❺ On the back of the time line, tell which events you chose and explain the connection you made with them.

Problem Chain

What you'll need:

Problem Chain sheet (page 37)

Grading Criteria

Setting	5 points
Characters and description	10 points
Problem/solution links	15 points
Solution summary	5 points
Life-changing problem	5 points
Followed directions	5 points
Neatness	5 points
	50 points

Steps:

❶ As you read a chapter in your novel, complete the appropriate section on the Problem Chain sheet. Use the back of the sheet if you need more room for chapter entries.

❷ When you finish the book, write a brief summary of the book ending.

❸ Write a sentence telling which problem faced by the character was the most life changing. On the back of the sheet, write an explanation.

Adventure

Novel News

What you'll need:

Novel News sheet (page 38), construction paper, samples of front pages of several newspapers

Steps:

1 Use the Novel News sheet to write a summary of the plot of your book in the style of a newspaper article.

2 On the construction paper, create the front page of a newspaper about your book. Use the sample newspapers as models. Decide what your headline will be, and then add your newspaper article.

3 Include a section with a brief description of the weather. This should relate to the weather that appeared most frequently in your novel.

4 Include an advertisement for the adventure featured in your novel.

Grading Criteria

News story	15 points
Adventure ad	10 points
Weather report	5 points
Graphics	5 points
Layout	5 points
Creativity	5 points
Neatness	5 points
	50 points

Story Map

What you'll need:

Adventure Story Map sheet (page 39)

Steps:

Complete the Story Map.

Grading Criteria

Event explanations	20 points
Setting identification	5 points
Problem identification	5 points
Solution identification	5 points
Followed directions	5 points
Mechanics	5 points
Neatness	5 points
	50 points

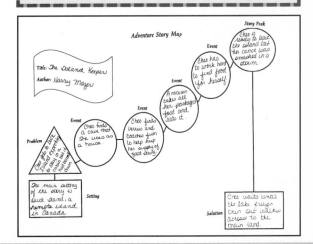

Character Journal Entries

Adventure

What you'll need:

colored pencils or markers, stapler

Steps:

1 Choose a character from your book.

2 Write ten journal entries describing the experiences of that character in your novel. Write your entries from the point of view of your character. Each entry needs to be at least one page long. Make sure you include a date on each of your entries.

3 Create a cover for your journal that includes the book's title and author's name.

4 Add illustrations to the cover that relate to the book and your character.

5 Staple the cover and pages together to form a book.

Grading Criteria

Organization	10 points
Adequate supporting details	10 points
Length requirement	10 points
Followed directions	5 points
Cover design	5 points
Mechanics	5 points
Neatness	5 points
	50 points

Setting Map

What you'll need:

9-by-18-inch sheet of white construction paper, colored pens or markers, five index cards, ruler

Steps:

1 Think about all the different places your character went throughout your book. On the construction paper, make a map that illustrates the different locations in the story. Label each place.

2 Write the title and the author of your book somewhere on the map.

3 Include a route that shows the order in which the character visited each place.

4 Write five questions on index cards that you could ask someone to answer about your map. Write the answers on the reverse side.

5 Make sure you include a map key and a compass rose.

Grading Criteria

Organization	10 points
Followed directions	10 points
Map route and labels	15 points
Questions/answers	5 points
Map key/compass rose	5 points
Neatness	5 points
	50 points

Adventure Brochure

What you'll need:

colored pens or markers, glue, old magazines that can be cut up, scissors

Steps:

1 Imagine you are setting up an adventure like the one that took place in your novel. Create a brochure that would make people interested in going on the adventure. The brochure should include information about the location, organized activities that are available, skills people will learn, sleeping/eating/bathing facilities, and any special features of the location. It should be informative and colorful.

2 Turn a sheet of paper horizontally so the paper is longest from left to right.

3 Fold the left third of the paper toward the middle.

4 Fold the right third of the paper backward toward the middle to make a trifold brochure.

5 Draw and/or cut out pictures for your brochure. Write a caption for each drawing or picture.

Grading Criteria	
Organization	10 points
Adequate details	15 points
Followed directions	10 points
Mechanics	5 points
Colorful	5 points
Neatness	5 points
	50 points

Conflict Chart

What you'll need:

Conflict Chart sheet (page 40)

Steps:

❶ Complete the Conflict Chart. Provide as many examples from the story as you can for each conflict type.

❷ On the back of your sheet, tell which of the conflicts was the most important to the story and explain why.

Grading Criteria

Conflict examples	20 points
Adequate supporting details	15 points
Explanation	5 points
Mechanics	5 points
Neatness	5 points
	50 points

Conflict Chart — Adventure

Name _Peter_   Date _Nov. 24_

Book Title: _Hatchet_

Author: _Gary Paulsen_

Person vs. Self – The character faces struggles against his or her own emotions, conscience, or physical limitations.
Person vs. Person – The character struggles against another character.
Person vs. Society – The character struggles against something presented by society or against a representative of society.
Person vs. Nature – The character struggles against a force of nature.
Person vs. Unknown – The character struggles against an unknown force.
Person vs. Object/Tool – The character struggles against an object or tool.

❖ Identify as many examples as possible from your novel for each type of conflict.

Person vs. Self
Brian is confused and angry about the divorce.

Person vs. Person
Brian is angry with his mother and won't speak to her.

Person vs. Society

Person vs. Nature
The porcupine attacks Brian with its quills.

Person vs. Unknown

Person vs. Object/Tool

Life Connections

What you'll need:

Life Connections sheet (page 41)

Grading Criteria

Quotes from the novel	20 points
Quotation connection	20 points
Adequate details	5 points
Neatness	5 points
	50 points

Steps:

❶ Complete the Life Connections sheet by choosing four quotes or parts of the novel that you can connect to your own life. Write the quotes in the speech balloons.

❷ Explain your connection to each of the quotes. Write your explanations in the boxes.

Name _____ Date _____

Book Title: _____

Author: _____

Main Characters

Setting

Chapter
Problem:
Solution:

Chapter
Problem:
Solution:

Chapter
Problem:
Solution:

Chapter
Problem:
Solution:

Chapter
Problem:
Solution:

Chapter
Problem:
Solution:

Summary

Life-Changing Problem

Name _____ Date _____

Book Title: _____

Author: _____

Answer the five W questions about your adventure book.

Who:

What:

When:

Where:

Why:

Now write a summary using the answers to your questions.

Story Map

Adventure

Name _____

Date _____

Title:

Author:

Story Peak

Event

Event

Event

Event

Solution

Problem

Setting

Name _____ Date _____

Book Title:_____

Author:_____

Person vs. Self – The character faces struggles against his or her own emotions, conscience, or physical limitations.

Person vs. Person – The character struggles against another character.

Person vs. Society – The character struggles against something presented by society or against a representative of society.

Person vs. Nature – The character struggles against a force of nature.

Person vs. Unknown – The character struggles against an unknown force.

Person vs. Object/Tool – The character struggles against an object or tool.

❖ **Identify as many examples as possible from your novel for each type of conflict.**

(**Person vs. Self**)

(**Person vs. Person**)

(**Person vs. Society**)

(**Person vs. Nature**)

(**Person vs. Unknown**)

(**Person vs. Object/Tool**)

Life Connections ———————————— Adventure

Name _____ Date _____

Book Title:_____

Author:_____

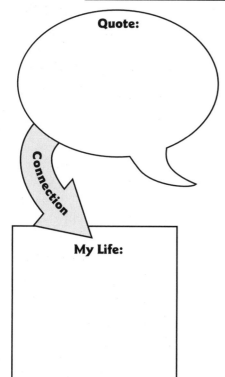

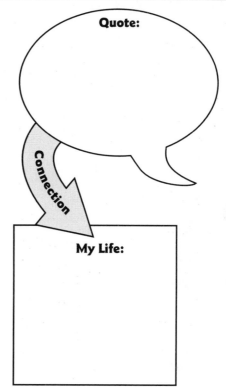

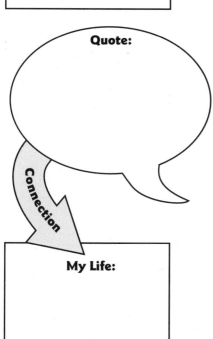

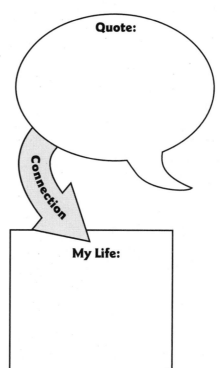

Grading Summary ———————————— Adventure

	Possible Score	My Score

☐ Event Time Line ....

Chronological order of events . . . . .15 points		_____
Event explanation . . . . .10 points		_____
Connections . . . . .10 points		_____
Followed directions . . . . .5 points		_____
Mechanics . . . . 5 points		_____
Neatness . . . . .5 points		_____
50 points		_____

☐ Problem Chain..

Setting . . . . .5 points		_____
Characters and description . . . . .10 points		_____
Problem/solution links . . . . .15 points		_____
Solution summary . . . . 5 points		_____
Life-changing problem . . . . 5 points		_____
Followed directions . . . . 5 points		_____
Neatness . . . . 5 points		_____
50 points		_____

☐ Novel News ....

News story . . . . .15 points		_____
Adventure ad . . . . .10 points		_____
Weather report . . . . .5 points		_____
Graphics . . . . .5 points		_____
Layout . . . . .5 points		_____
Creativity . . . . .5 points		_____
Neatness . . . . .5 points		_____
50 points		_____

☐ Story Map ....

Event explanations . . . . .20 points		_____
Setting identification . . . . .5 points		_____
Problem identification . . . . .5 points		_____
Solution identification . . . . .5 points		_____
Followed directions . . . . 5 points		_____
Mechanics . . . . 5 points		_____
Neatness . . . . 5 points		_____
50 points		_____

Grading Summary ——————————— Adventure

	Possible Score	**My Score**

☐ Character Journal Entries

	Possible Score	My Score
Organization	10 points	_____
Adequate supporting details	10 points	_____
Length requirement	10 points	_____
Followed directions	5 points	_____
Cover design	5 points	_____
Mechanics	5 points	_____
Neatness	5 points	_____
	50 points	_____

☐ Setting Map

	Possible Score	My Score
Organization	10 points	_____
Followed directions	10 points	_____
Map route and labels	15 points	_____
Questions/answers	5 points	_____
Map key/compass rose	5 points	_____
Neatness	5 points	_____
	50 points	_____

☐ Adventure Brochure

	Possible Score	My Score
Organization	10 points	_____
Adequate details	15 points	_____
Followed directions	10 points	_____
Mechanics	5 points	_____
Colorful	5 points	_____
Neatness	5 points	_____
	50 points	_____

☐ Conflict Chart

	Possible Score	My Score
Conflict examples	20 points	_____
Adequate supporting details	15 points	_____
Explanation	5 points	_____
Mechanics	5 points	_____
Neatness	5 points	_____
	50 points	_____

☐ Life Connections

	Possible Score	My Score
Quotes from the novel	20 points	_____
Quotation connection	20 points	_____
Adequate details	5 points	_____
Neatness	5 points	_____
	50 points	_____

Total for all three projects _____

Fairy Tale Projects

Name _____   Due Date _____

Book Title: _____

✦ Make a tic-tac-toe by choosing three projects to complete for your novel.

Time Traveler	**Puppet Play** (Partner)	**Story Map**
Pack Your Trunk	**Scene Collage**	**Talk Show Interview** (Partner)
Wanted Poster	**Design a Magic Object**	**Similarity & Difference Chart**

Time Traveler

What you'll need:

Time Traveler sheet (page 50), colored pencils or markers

Grading Criteria	
Paragraphs	20 points
Setting illustration	20 points
Followed directions	5 points
Mechanics	5 points
	50 points

Steps:

❶ On the Time Traveler sheet, fill in the actual setting information based on your fairy tale. Make sure you use specific examples from the story.

❷ Then, create a new setting for the story. List the new setting information on the sheet.

❸ Draw a picture of the setting on a sheet of unlined paper.

❹ On lined paper, write a paragraph explaining how the new setting would affect the character and the story plot. Your paragraph should be half a page, typed. Use specific examples from the story.

❺ Decide which setting you would rather live in. Write a paragraph explaining your choice.

Puppet Play

What you'll need:

paper towel roll tubes, yarn, paper, clay, scraps of cloth

Grading Criteria	
Organization	10 points
Followed directions	10 points
Adequate details	10 points
Puppet	10 points
Presentation	10 points
	50 points

Steps:

❶ Choose one or two partners to work with.

❷ Decide on a scene from a fairy tale. Rewrite the scene as a script for a puppet play.

❸ When you've completed your script, make a puppet. The puppet can be made out of any type of material, so be as creative as possible.

❹ Turn your script in to your teacher before the due date so it can be approved before you perform your play.

Story Map

What you'll need:

9-by-18-inch sheet of white construction paper, colored pencils or markers

Steps:

❶ Design a story map for your fairy tale. Make sure you include:

- Setting
- Characters
- Problem
- Five events—draw a line to show their connection and put the events in order
- Climax
- Solution

❷ Write a paragraph that explains your story map on another sheet of paper.

❸ Illustrate your story map with images from your fairy tale. For example, if your story has castles, unicorns, and wizards, you should incorporate them into your map design.

Grading Criteria	
Story Map design	5 points
Event identification	5 points
Setting identification	5 points
Problem identification	5 points
Solution identification	5 points
Paragraph	5 points
Creativity	5 points
Followed directions	5 points
Mechanics	5 points
Neat/colorful	5 points
	50 points

Pack Your Trunk

What you'll need:

9-by-18-inch sheet of white construction paper, paper lunch sack, colored pencils or markers

Grading Criteria	
Explanation	15 points
Character objects	10 points
Presentation	10 points
Followed directions	5 points
Creativity	5 points
Neat/colorful	5 points
	50 points

Steps:

❶ Make a list of ten items that represent your character. Then write a few sentences about each item, telling what each item says about the character and where the item first appears in the story.

❷ Draw and color a picture of each item. Put your items in the paper sack "trunk" and write the character's name on the outside.

❸ Practice talking about each item because you will have to present these items to the class along with your explanation of their importance to your character.

❹ Present your items to the class when your project is due.

Scene Collage

What you'll need:

9-by-18-inch sheet of white construction paper, colored pencils or markers, glue, materials such as tissue paper, foil, yarn, photos from old magazines

Grading Criteria	
Collage picture	15 points
Paragraph	15 points
Creativity	10 points
Followed directions	5 points
Neatness	5 points
	50 points

Steps:

❶ Choose a scene from your fairy tale.

❷ Create a collage illustrating your scene by gluing various materials like tissue paper, foil, yarn, construction paper, and magazine pictures on the large sheet of construction paper.

❸ Use lined paper to write a short paragraph telling about the scene, where in the fairy tale it occurs, and why you chose this particular scene. Glue this page to the bottom of your scene.

❹ Finally add the fairy tale's title.

Fairy Tales

Talk Show Interview

What you'll need:

a costume for dressing up as a character from your fairy tale

Grading Criteria	
Talk-show style	15 points
Questions	10 points
Presentation	10 points
Creativity	10 points
Followed directions	5 points
	50 points

Steps:

❶ With a partner, choose a character that you would like to interview.

❷ Write a list of ten questions that the interviewer would ask the character. (Turn these in to your teacher for preapproval before the due date.)

❸ On presentation day, one of you will be the interviewer and the other the character. Make sure you introduce the interviewer and the character at the beginning of the segment.

❹ To make it more authentic, the character should come in costume.

❺ Practice the interview at home before performing it in class.

Wanted Poster

What you'll need:

9-by-18-inch sheet of white construction paper, colored pencils or markers

Grading Criteria	
Adequate details	20 points
Layout	10 points
Followed directions	10 points
Mechanics	5 points
Neat/colorful	5 points
	50 points

Steps:

❶ Use the construction paper to make a Wanted Poster for the villain in your fairy tale. The layout of your poster is important, so plan the design before you begin drawing it.

❷ Your poster must include the following:

- The character's name
- A picture of the character
- A physical description of the character
- Reason he or she is wanted
- Location where the character was last seen
- A reward amount

Wanted

The Big Bad Wolf

The wolf has dark brown fur, beady eyes, pointy ears, a long red tongue and a big mouth.

The wolf is wanted for eating the first and second little pigs.

Design a Magic Object

— Fairy Tales

What you'll need:

colored pencils or markers

Steps:

❶ Decide on a magic object that the character in your fairy tale could have used to protect him- or herself from the villain.

❷ Draw and color the object.

❸ Beneath your drawing, write a paragraph describing the object.

Grading Criteria

Object drawing	10 points
Adequate details	10 points
Written paragraph	10 points
Followed directions	5 points
Creativity	5 points
Mechanics	5 points
Neatness	5 points
	50 points

Similarty & Difference Chart

What you'll need:

9-by-18-inch sheet of white construction paper, colored pencils or markers, ruler

Steps:

❶ Draw two squares (one on the right side and one on the left side of the construction paper).

❷ In each square, draw a picture of a main character in the fairy tale. Label each drawing.

❸ In between the two squares, draw horizontal lines. Use them to write the similarities between the two characters.

❹ Around the outside of each square, tell how the characters are different.

❺ Provide as many similarities and differences as you can. Be specific and use examples from the story.

Grading Criteria

Similarity retelling	15 points
Difference retelling	15 points
Followed directions	5 points
Organization	10 points
Neatness	5 points
	50 points

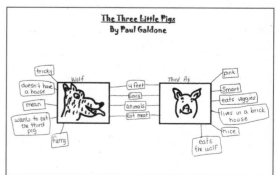

Name _____ Date _____

Current Setting

Time:

Place:

Mood:

New Setting

Time:

Place:

Mood:

❖ **Draw a picture of the new setting on a separate sheet of paper. Make sure it is neat and colorful.**

❖ **Write a paragraph telling how the new setting will affect the main character and the story plot.**

❖ **Write another paragraph telling which setting you would rather live in and why.**

Fantasy

haracter Web

t you'll need:

aracter Web sheet (page 62)

:

Write the name of the main character from
your novel in the center circle on the
Character Web sheet. In each of the boxes,
ist one characteristic or quality of the
haracter's personality.

On the back of the sheet, write a statement
or event from the story that supports each
haracteristic or quality you listed.

Grading Criteria	
Organization	15 points
Followed directions	10 points
Adequate supporting details	15 points
Mechanics	5 points
Neatness	5 points
	50 points

Character Web ——————————————————— **Fantasy**

ame **Nick**   Date **3/27**

omplete the Character Web by listing one characteristic or quality of your character's personality in each square. On the back of this sheet,
..ite a statement or action from the story that supports your choices.

Funny   6.   Brave   1.

Generous   5.   **Harry Potter**   2.   Smart

Loyal   4.   3.   Kind

Grading Summary ——————————————————— **Fairy Tales**

	Possible Score	My Score
☐ **Time Traveler**		
Paragraphs	20 points	_____
Setting illustration	20 points	_____
Followed directions	5 points	_____
Mechanics	5 points	_____
	50 points	_____
☐ **Puppet Play**		
Organization	10 points	_____
Followed directions	10 points	_____
Adequate details	10 points	_____
Puppet	10 points	_____
Presentation	10 points	_____
	50 points	_____
☐ **Story Map**		
Story map design	5 points	_____
Event identification	5 points	_____
Setting identification	5 points	_____
Problem identification	5 points	_____
Solution identification	5 points	_____
Paragraph	5 points	_____
Creativity	5 points	_____
Followed directions	5 points	_____
Mechanics	5 points	_____
Neat/colorful	5 points	_____
	50 points	_____
☐ **Pack Your Trunk**		
Explanation	15 points	_____
Character objects	10 points	_____
Presentation	10 points	_____
Followed directions	5 points	_____
Creativity	5 points	_____
Neat/colorful	5 points	_____
	50 points	_____

Grading Summary ———————— **Fairy Tales**

	Possible Score	My Score

❑ **Scene Collage** ....

Collage picture . . . . .15 points		_____
Paragraph . . . . .15 points		_____
Creativity . . . . .10 points		_____
Followed directions . . . . .5 points		_____
Neatness . . . . .5 points		_____
50 points		_____

❑ **Talk Show Interview** ....

Talk-show style . . . . 15 points		_____
Questions . . . . .10 points		_____
Presentation . . . . .10 points		_____
Creativity . . . . .10 points		_____
Followed directions . . . . .5 points		_____
50 points		_____

❑ **Wanted Poster** ....

Adequate details . . . . .20 points		_____
Layout . . . . .15 points		_____
Followed directions . . . . .5 points		_____
Mechanics . . . . .5 points		_____
Neat/colorful . . . . .5 points		_____
50 points		_____

❑ **Design a Magic Object** ....

Object drawing . . . . .10 points		_____
Adequate details . . . . .10 points		_____
Written paragraph . . . . .10 points		_____
Followed directions . . . . .5 points		_____
Creativity . . . . .5 points		_____
Mechanics . . . . .5 points		_____
Neat/colorful . . . . .5 points		_____
50 points		_____

❑ **Similarity & Difference Chart** ....

Similarity retelling . . . . .15 points		_____
Difference retelling . . . . .15 points		_____
Followed directions . . . . .5 points		_____
Organization . . . . 10 points		_____
Neatness . . . . .5 points		_____
50 points		_____

Total for all three projects _____

Fantasy Projects

Name _____ Due Date _____

Book Title: _____

✦ Make a tic-tac-toe by choosing three projects to complete for your no

Character Web	Event Comparison	Plan a
Prediction Chain	Gold Star Book Award	Fant Jou
Write an Editorial	Reality & Make-Believe Chart	St M

Event Comparison

What you'll need:

Event Comparison sheet (page 63)

Steps:

❶ List six important events from your novel on the Event Comparison sheet.

❷ Compare each one event in the story to an event in your own life. Tell how the event is the same as or different from experiences you have had.

Grading Criteria	
Adequate details	20 points
Organization	15 points
Followed directions	5 points
Mechanics	5 points
Neatness	5 points
	50 points

Event Comparison ———————————— **Fantasy**

Name Ama   Date Feb. 25

Event One:
Harry's parents die. He is forced to live with his aunt and uncle.

> **Real-life Comparison**
> When my mom and dad go out of town, I have to stay at my grandparents.

Event Four:
Harry is very good at Quidditch and joins the team.

> **Real-life Comparison**
> I'm very good at dancing. I plan to join the dance team.

Event Two:
Harry gets an invitation to attend Hogwarts. His family doesn't think he should go. He goes anyway.

> **Real-life Comparison**
> I got an invitation to a sleepover party. My parents didn't want me to go. I talked them into letting me.

Event Five:
Harry stays at Hogwarts for Christmas.

> **Real-life Comparison**
> We weren't home for Christmas one year. We had to go to a wedding that was far away.

Event Three:
Harry meets Ron on his way to Hogwarts.

> **Real-life Comparison**
> I met my best friend Elaine on the first day of school.

Event Six
Harry goes into the forbidden forest.

> **Real-life Comparison**
> Once I got lost in a state park. It was really scary.

Plan a Trip

Grading Criteria

Adequate details	15 points
Creativity	15 points
Organization	5 points
Followed directions	5 points
Mechanics	5 points
Neatness	5 points
	50 points

What you'll need:

small sheet of construction paper, stapler, colored pencils or markers

Steps:

❶ After you have read your novel, create a trip journal for a trip similar to the one that the main character went on.

❷ On the first page of your journal, present an outline of the imaginary trip. The following questions can help you get started, but you can add any other information that is important to your trip.

  ✳ Where do you plan to go?

  ✳ How are you going to get to your destination?

  ✳ Who is going with you?

  ✳ What do you plan to see?

  ✳ How much money do you have for your trip?

❸ Write journal entries for ten days of your adventure—one entry per page. Each journal entry should be at least three-quarters of a page. Make sure you put a heading on each entry.

❹ Create a cover for your journal. Be sure to include the title of your book and the author's name. Add illustrations to the cover that reflect the content of the book.

My Trip to the Forbidden Forest

by Jordan

Prediction Chain

Grading Criteria

Adequate prediction details	15 points
Followed directions	10 points
Rating and self-reflection	5 points
Organization	5 points
Ending retelling	5 points
Mechanics	5 points
Neatness	5 points
	50 points

What you'll need:

9-by-18-inch sheet of white construction paper, colored pencils or markers

Steps:

❶ Draw a 2-inch square in the top left-hand corner of the construction paper.

❷ Write the title and author of your novel in the square.

❸ Each time you finish reading a chapter, draw a circle on your paper and write the chapter number and a prediction about the next chapter. Put a star in the circle if you determine your prediction was correct after you finish reading that chapter.

❹ Continue this process until you finish the novel. Draw a line to link your circles together to make a chain.

❺ In the last circle, retell how the story ends.

❻ On the back of your sheet rate your prediction skills from 1 (poor) to 5 (excellent).

❼ Tell why you rated yourself the way you did.

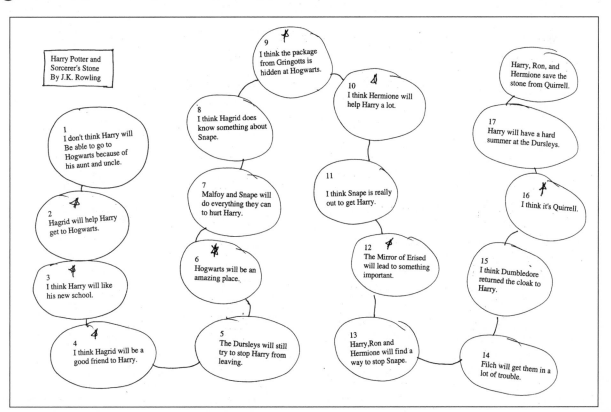

Gold Star Book Award

What you'll need:

colored pencils or markers

Steps:

❶ Create a certificate or a ribbon that could be given as an award to the author of your book.

❷ Write a paragraph explaining why you recommend this book for the Gold Star Book Award. Your paragraph should include information that answers the following questions:

✱ Why did you like the book?

✱ Was the story believable?

✱ Were the characters realistic?

✱ Did the description of the setting seem accurate?

✱ What was the mood of the story (funny, sad, both)?

Grading Criteria	
Creativity	15 points
Adequate details	10 points
Recommendation	10 points
Followed directions	5 points
Mechanics	5 points
Neat/colorful	5 points
	50 points

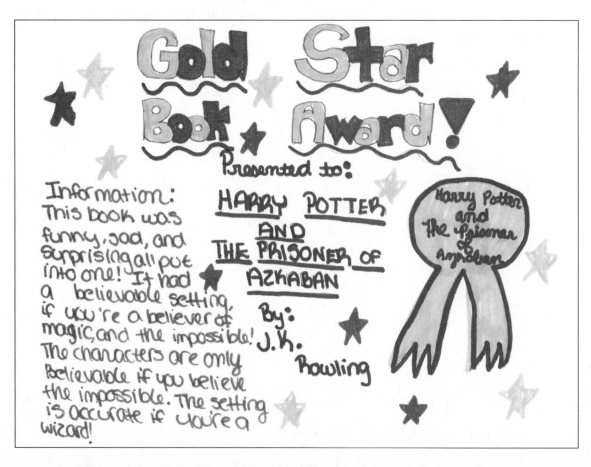

Gold Star Book Award!

Presented to: HARRY POTTER AND THE PRISONER OF AZKABAN

By: J.K. Rowling

Information: This book was funny, sad, and surprising all put into one! It had a believable setting, if you're a believer of magic, and the impossible! The characters are only believable if you believe the impossible. The setting is accurate if you're a wizard!

Harry Potter and the Prisoner of Azkaban

Fantasy Journal

What you'll need:

stapler, colored pencils or markers

Grading Criteria

Adequate details	20 points
Creativity	15 points
Followed directions	5 points
Mechanics	5 points
Neatness	5 points
	50 points

Steps:

❶ Create a journal by folding five sheets of unlined white paper in half horizontally. Staple the journal together along the fold.

❷ On the cover of the journal, write the book's title and the author's name.

❸ Write journal entries, one per page, in response to the following prompts:

✳ Describe the setting. Tell how it is the same as and different from where you live. Illustrate it.

✳ Describe one element of the book that makes it clear it is a fantasy.

✳ List any questions that occur to you while reading the novel. If they get answered, come back and write down the answers.

✳ Write about how one character feels. Tell about a time you felt the same way.

✳ Describe two characters. Tell how one of these characters is the same as or different from you. Draw illustrations of them.

✳ Describe one of the situations a character faces. Tell about a time you were faced with a similar situation.

✳ Write down a quote from the book that is meaningful to you. Tell why you chose this quote.

✳ Describe the climax (high point) of the story. Then tell why you think this is the high point.

✳ List ten major events from the story in order from beginning to end. Use complete sentences. Put a star by the most important event and tell why you chose this event.

✳ Tell about an event from the story that is similar to something that happened to you. Describe your event. Explain how the two events relate.

Write an Editorial

Steps:

An editorial is an article in a newspaper or magazine that expresses the opinion of the editor or publisher. Write an editorial about an issue or event from your novel. The article must express your opinion about the issue. The issue should be important to the story plot. The

article should be three-quarters of a page if typed or one page if hand-written. You may want to do a little research on editorials by reading newspaper editorials for several days.

Grading Criteria	
Adequate details	20 points
Creativity	15 points
Followed directions	5 points
Mechanics	5 points
Neatness	5 points
	50 points

Reality & Make-Believe Chart

What you'll need:

Reality and Make-Believe Chart sheet (page 64)

Steps:

❶ Find three events from your book that could happen in real life: one from the beginning, one from the middle, and one from the end of the story. Record these events on your chart.

❷ Find three events from the beginning, middle, and end of your story that are make believe. Record these events on your chart.

❸ Write a paragraph on the back of the sheet telling which of these events you would like to have happen to you. Explain your answer.

Grading Criteria	
Real events	15 points
Make-believe events	15 points
Written paragraph	10 points
Followed directions	5 points
Mechanics	5 points
	50 points

Fantasy

Story Map

What you'll need:

9-by-18-inch white construction paper, colored pencils or markers

Steps:

❶ You are going to design your own story map. Make sure you include:
   ✳ Setting
   ✳ Characters
   ✳ Problem
   ✳ Eight Events

❷ Write a paragraph telling about your story map.

❸ Make sure your design includes key concepts from your novel. For example, if your story has castles, unicorns, and wizards, you should incorporate them into your map design.

❹ Make sure your map is creative and colorful.

Grading Criteria	
Story map design	5 points
Event identification	5 points
Setting identification	5 points
Problem identification	5 points
Paragraph	10 points
Creativity	5 points
Followed directions	5 points
Mechanics	5 points
Neat/colorful	5 points
	50 points

Setting

castle

8 Events

1. Harry Potter finds out that his parents were killed by a curse.
2. He gets an invitation to attend Hogwarts
3. He goes and meets his 2 friends, Ron Weasley, and Hermione Granger
4. While at the bank, Harry finds out Hogwarts is hiding something
5. They find out it's the Sorcerer's Stone

6. Lord Voldemort is back and wants Harry
7. Harry finds the room where the stone is being hid
8. He saves the stone, and defeats Lord Voldemort again

Characters
Harry Hermione Ron Voldemort
Hagrid Dumbledore

Problem

There was many problems throughout the book. The main one is that there is a precious stone being held at Hogwarts. There is an evil wizard that is after the stone and it is up to Harry and company to figure it out.

Paragraph

Where Harry Potter finds out he is going to Hogwarts, he is happy until he finds out Lord Voldemort is after him. then he and his friends find out Lord Voldemort is after the Sorcerer's Stone. They find out where it is hid, and save it.

Character Web ——————— Fantasy

Name _____

Date _____

Complete the character web by listing one characteristic or quality of your character's personality in each box. On the back of this sheet, write a statement or action from the story that supports your choices.

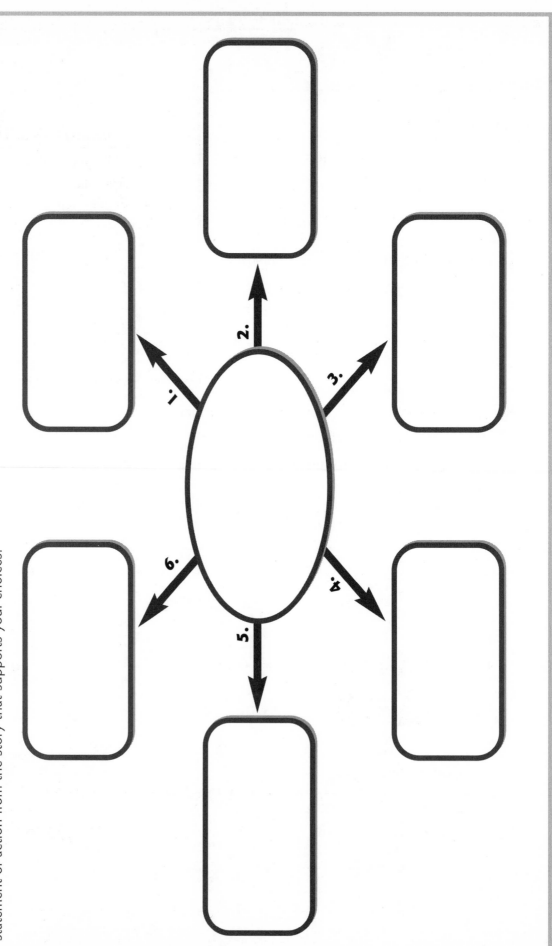

Event Comparison ——————————————— Fantasy

Name _____ Date _____

Event One:

_____
_____
_____
_____
_____
_____

> **Real-Life Comparison**

Event Two:

_____
_____
_____
_____
_____
_____

> **Real-Life Comparison**

Event Three:

_____
_____
_____
_____
_____

> **Real-Life Comparison**

Event Four:

_____
_____
_____
_____
_____
_____

> **Real-Life Comparison**

Event Five:

_____
_____
_____
_____
_____
_____

> **Real-Life Comparison**

Event Six

_____
_____
_____
_____
_____

> **Real-Life Comparison**

Name _____ Date _____

	Reality	Make Believe
Beginning		
Middle		
End		

Grading Summary ———————————— Fantasy

	Possible Score	My Score

☐ Character Web ....

Organization	.15 points	_____
Followed directions	.10 points	_____
Adequate supporting details	.15 points	_____
Mechanics	5 points	_____
Neatness	.5 points	_____
	50 points	_____

☐ Event Comparison ....

Adequate details	.20 points	_____
Organization	.15 points	_____
Followed directions	.5 points	_____
Mechanics	.5 points	_____
Neatness	5 points	_____
	50 points	_____

☐ Plan a Trip ....

Adequate details	.15 points	_____
Creativity	.15 points	_____
Organization	.5 points	_____
Followed directions	.5 points	_____
Mechanics	.5 points	_____
Neatness	5 points	_____
	50 points	_____

☐ Prediction Chain ....

Adequate prediction details	.15 points	_____
Followed directions	.10 points	_____
Rating and self-reflection	.5 points	_____
Organization	.5 points	_____
Ending retelling	.5 points	_____
Mechanics	.5 points	_____
Neat/colorful	.5 points	_____
	50 points	_____

☐ Gold Star Book Award ....

Creativity	.15 points	_____
Adequate details	.10 points	_____
Recommendation	.10 points	_____
Followed directions	.5 points	_____
Mechanics	5 points	_____
Neatness	.5 points	_____
	50 points	_____

Grading Summary ——————————— Fantasy

	Possible Score	My Score

❑ Fantasy Journal ....

	Possible Score	My Score
Adequate details	.20 points	_____
Creativity	.15 points	_____
Followed directions	.5 points	_____
Mechanics	.5 points	_____
Neatness	. 5 points	_____
	50 points	_____

❑ Write an Editorial ....

	Possible Score	My Score
Adequate details	.20 points	_____
Creativity	.15 points	_____
Followed directions	.5 points	_____
Mechanics	.5 points	_____
Neatness	. 5 points	_____
	50 points	_____

❑ Reality & Make-believe Chart ....

	Possible Score	My Score
Real events	.15 points	_____
Make-believe events	.15 points	_____
Written paragraph	.10 points	_____
Followed directions	. 5 points	_____
Mechanics	.5 points	_____
	50 points	_____

❑ Story Map ....

	Possible Score	My Score
Story map design	. 5 points	_____
Event identification	.5 points	_____
Setting identification	.5 points	_____
Problem identification	.5 points	_____
Paragraph	.10 points	_____
Creativity	.5 points	_____
Followed directions	.5 points	_____
Mechanics	.5 points	_____
Neat/colorful	.5 points	_____
	50 points	_____

Total for all three projects _____

Realistic Fiction Projects

Name _____ Due Date _____

Book Title: _____

✦ Make a tic-tac-toe by choosing three projects to complete for your novel.

Setting Identification	**Character Trait Chart**	**Character Poster**
Before and After	**Book Parts**	**Fact and Opinion**
Connections	**Diary Entries**	**Character Feeling Chart**

Setting Identification

What you'll need:

colored pencils or markers

Steps:

1 At the top of a sheet of unlined white paper, write the name of your book and its author.

2 Below this, identify the setting of your book.

3 Then, list three clues that helped you identify the setting of the story.

4 Write a paragraph explaining how the setting was important to the story.

5 Draw an illustration of the setting below the paragraph.

Grading Criteria	
Identified setting	10 points
Written paragraph	10 points
Three setting clues	10 points
Adequate details	10 points
Followed directions	5 points
Mechanics	5 points
	50 points

Character Trait Chart

What you'll need:

Character Trait Chart sheet (page 73)

Steps:

1 Choose three characters from your book.

2 As you read the book, use the Character Trait Chart sheet to keep a record of the traits each character possesses.

3 Support each trait you choose with a passage from your book.

Grading Criteria	
Adequate supporting details	15 points
Trait explanations	10 points
Organization	10 points
Followed directions	5 points
Mechanics	5 points
Neatness	5 points
	50 points

Character Poster

What you'll need:

9-by-18-inch sheet of white construction paper, colored pencils or markers

Steps:

❶ Choose a character from your book.

❷ Use information from the book to draw and color a picture of your character on the construction paper. Add a label with the character's name.

❸ Around the outside of the character, draw six circles or shapes in which to write information about the character. You can write about the character's friends, conflicts, feelings, personality traits, and appearance. Think of one more category that would help you share important information about your character.

❹ On the back of your Character Poster, explain one connection you can make with the character.

Grading Criteria

Illustration	10 points
Adequate supporting details	15 points
Connection	10 points
Organization	5 points
Followed directions	5 points
Neat/colorful	5 points
	50 points

Before and After

What you'll need:

9-by-18-inch sheet of white construction paper, colored pencils or markers, index cards, glue

Grading Criteria

Illustration	15 points
Adequate supporting details	10 points
Paragraphs	15 points
Followed directions	5 points
Neat/colorful	5 points
	50 points

Steps:

❶ Select a passage from the book. Then draw and color a picture on the construction paper based on the passage.

❷ On an index card, write a description to go with your picture. Glue the description to the bottom of the picture.

❸ On another sheet of paper, write a paragraph telling about what happened before the scene you've illustrated, and another paragraph telling what happened after the scene.

Book Parts

What you'll need:

Book Parts sheet (page 74)

Grading Criteria

Adequate supporting details	20 points
Personal reaction	25 points
Followed directions	5 points
	50 points

Steps:

❶ Use the Book Parts sheet to describe a situation or event from your book that fits with each heading (Saddest, Funniest, Most Unbelievable, Most Embarrassing, Happiest).

❷ On another sheet of paper, write a paragraph giving your personal reaction to each of these parts.

Book Parts ——————————————— Realistic Fiction

Name: *Cyrus* Date: *March 12*
Book Title: *The Outsiders* Author: *S.E. Hinton*

Saddest Part	The saddest part of the book was when Johnny died after saving the children from the burning church.
Funniest Part	The funniest part of The Outsiders was when Cherry Valance touched the coke Dallas brought her into his face.
Most Unbelievable Part	The most unbelievable part was when Johnny knifed Bob, the Soc, and killed him.
Most Embarrassing Part	An embarrassing moment for Ponyboy is when he starts crying after he realizes that Johnny killed the Soc.
Happiest Part	The end of the story is going to start a happier chapter in Ponyboy's life. He realizes where he wants to be when he gets older.

─── **Realistic Fiction**

Fact and Opinion

What you'll need:

Fact and Opinion sheet (page 75)

Steps:

1 At the top of the Fact and Opinion sheet, write down ten different statements made by the main character.

2 On the bottom of the sheet, sort the statements into facts and opinions by listing the number of each statement under the appropriate column.

3 On the back of the sheet, tell which of these statements you think is the most important and explain why you feel this way.

Grading Criteria	
Sorting of statements	25 points
Explanation	15 points
Organization	5 points
Followed directions	5 points
	50 points

Connections

Steps:

1 On a sheet of paper, describe three situations from the book that you can connect with situations you—or people you know—have been in. Be sure to:

✱ Describe the book situation.

✱ Give the name of the person with whom the situation connects.

✱ Include specific details when explaining how the person and the situation are connected.

Grading Criteria	
Adequate supporting details	15 points
Description paragraph	10 points
Connections	10 points
Organization	10 points
Followed directions	5 points
	50 points

Connections

1. *Johnny and Ponyboy go into the burning church to save the children that where trapped inside.*
   ◆ *I saved a kitten one time when it crawled up into one of our apple trees and couldn't get back down.*

2. *Johnny likes to read books.*
   ◆ *In my spare time I also like to read. I have a hard time putting my books done sometimes.*

3. *Johnny has two older brothers. His oldest brother, Darry, is the head of the family since their parents were killed in an automobile accident. He has a good relationship with his second brother.*
   ◆ *I also have two older brothers. I also get along better with my second brother.*

Diary Entries

What you'll need:

sheet of construction paper, colored pencils or markers, stapler

Grading Criteria

Five diary accounts	20 points
Reasons	10 points
Organization	10 points
Journal design	5 points
Followed directions	5 points
	50 points

Steps:

❶ Imagine you are one of the main characters in your book.

❷ Design a diary for the character to write daily entries. Fold three sheets of unlined paper in half like a book. Make a cover with the construction paper and then staple along the fold.

❸ Write five diary accounts of the character's daily thoughts and activities. Choose important parts of the book from which to write your entries. Write the entry from the character's point of view.

❹ At the end of each entry, explain why you felt this was an important part of the story.

Character Feeling Chart

What you'll need:

Character Feeling Chart sheet (page 76)

Grading Criteria

Feeling details	20 points
Connection	15 points
Followed directions	10 points
Neatness	5 points
	50 points

Steps:

❶ After you've finished your book, complete the Character Feeling Chart sheet by writing the character's name at the top. Then, tell how the character felt at the beginning, the middle, and the end of the novel.

❷ Write about a time you felt like the character in the connections section. Be specific.

Character Feeling Chart ─────── Realistic Fiction

Name _Audrey_   Date _June 17, 2004_

Character's Name   _Ponyboy Curtis_

Beginning	Middle	End
Ponyboy is carefree. He is a good student. Things seem to come easy to him.	Ponyboy is scared. Johnny killed a Soc and Ponyboy had Johnny ran away to hide from the cops. Ponyboy was scared he would be sent to a foster home.	Ponyboy is sad but hopeful. He is sad because he's lost two of his friends, Johnny and Dallas. He is hopeful about the future.

Connections: Like Ponyboy, I feel hopeful about the future. I think it's better to look ahead instead of focusing on past mistakes.

Character Trait Chart ——————————————— Realistic Fiction

Name _____ Date _____

Character 1	Character 2	Character 3

Book Parts ——— Realistic Fiction

Name _____ Date _____

Book Title: _____

Author: _____

Saddest Part	
Funniest Part	
Most Unbelievable Part	
Most Embarrassing Part	
Happiest Part	

Fact and Opinion ———————————— Realistic Fiction

Name _____ Date _____

List ten statements made by the main character in your book.

1.

2.

3.

4.

5.

6.

7.

8.

9.

10.

Sort the statements you listed above into facts and opinions. List the number of each statement under the column where it fits.

Fact	Opinion

Character Feeling Chart ———— Realistic Fiction

Name _____

Date _____

Character's Name _____

Beginning	Middle	End

Connections:

Grading Summary ———————— Realistic Fiction

	Possible Score	My Score

☐ Setting Identification ....

	Possible Score	My Score
Identified setting	10 points	_____
Written paragraph	10 points	_____
Three setting clues	10 points	_____
Adequate details	10 points	_____
Followed directions	5 points	_____
Mechanics	5 points	_____
	50 points	_____

☐ Character Trait Chart ....

	Possible Score	My Score
Adequate supporting details	15 points	_____
Trait explanations	10 points	_____
Organization	10 points	_____
Followed directions	5 points	_____
Mechanics	5 points	_____
Neatness	5 points	_____
	50 points	_____

☐ Character Poster ....

	Possible Score	My Score
Illustration	10 points	_____
Adequate supporting details	15 points	_____
Connection	10 points	_____
Organization	5 points	_____
Followed directions	5 points	_____
Neat/colorful	5 points	_____
	50 points	_____

☐ Before and After ....

	Possible Score	My Score
Illustration	15 points	_____
Adequate supporting details	10 points	_____
Paragraphs	15 points	_____
Followed directions	5 points	_____
Neat/colorful	5 points	_____
	50 points	_____

☐ Book Parts ....

	Possible Score	My Score
Adequate supporting details	20 points	_____
Personal reaction	25 points	_____
Followed directions	5 points	_____
	50 points	_____

Grading Summary ———————————— Realistic Fiction

	Possible Score	**My Score**

❑ Fact and Opinion...

	Possible Score	My Score
Sorting of statements	.25 points	_____
Explanation	.15 points	_____
Organization	. 5 points	_____
Followed directions	.5 points	_____
	50 points	_____

❑ Connections...

	Possible Score	My Score
Adequate supporting details	.15 points	_____
Description paragraph	.10 points	_____
Connections	.10 points	_____
Organization	.10 points	_____
Followed directions	. 5 points	_____
	50 points	_____

❑ Diary Entries...

	Possible Score	My Score
Five diary accounts	.20 points	_____
Reasons	.10 points	_____
Organization	.10 points	_____
Journal design	.5 points	_____
Followed directions	. 5 points	_____
	50 points	_____

❑ Character Feeling Chart...

	Possible Score	My Score
Feeling details	.20 points	_____
Connection	.15 points	_____
Followed directions	.10 points	_____
Neatness	. 5 points	_____
	50 points	_____

Total for all three projects   _____

Biography Projects

Name _____ Due Date _____

Book Title: _____

✦ Make a tic-tac-toe by choosing three projects to complete for your novel.

Personal Development Chart	Book Jacket	Feelings Accordion Book
Book Talk	Children's Book	Memory Box
Write a Letter	Biography Map	Design a CD Cover

Personal Development Chart
Biography

What you'll need:

Personal Development Chart sheet (page 85)

Steps:

Follow the directions on the Personal Development Chart sheet.

Grading Criteria

Personal life details	20 points
Personal descriptions	10 points
Rating	5 points
Followed directions	5 points
Mechanics	5 points
Neatness	5 points
	50 points

Personal Development Chart
Directions: As you read your novel, complete the personal development chart.

Person's Name
Emma Edmonds

Behind Rebel Lines

Personal Description
Emma was twenty one. She was trim and boyish. She had short cropped hair like a man and blue eyes. She wore men's clothing.

Initial Feelings about person Chapters 1&2
My initial feelings about Emma was that she was brave and strong willed.

Personal Development Chapters 3 - 10
In the middle chapters Emma became a spy. She learned about different artillery and developed a wide variety of disguises that helped her penetrate the Confederate camps. While in these camps, she was able to learn valuable secrets that helped the North win major battles.

Personal Development Chapters 11 - 15
One of the biggest assignments that Emma had was to find an agent feeding information to the Confederate troops. She worked for weeks in Louisville to find the agent. She was able to slowly find the agent and help in his capture.

Ending Description of the Person
By the end of the book, Emma was a mother of three sons. She is plump and matronly. She wears women's clothing instead of dressing like a man.

How did the person change?
At the beginning of the biography, Emma was twenty one. At the end she was a mature woman with a husband and three sons. She turned into a plump, matronly lady that wore fancy bonnets and long skirts.

Person's Toughest Obstacle
Emma's toughest obstacle was to have Franklin Thompson, Emma's soldier name, declared an honorable discharge with full back pay. When Emma became sick she had to leave to get treatment so that she would not be found out. During this time she was considered a deserter.

Person Rating (Circle a Number)
1 low   2   3   4   ⑤ high

On the back tell why you rated your person this way.

Emma was very brave. The masterful disguises she used to fool the rebels were impressive. She took pride in her work.

Book Jacket

What you'll need:

9-by-18-inch sheet of white construction paper, ruler, colored pencils or markers

Grading Criteria

Organization	10 points
Illustrations	10 points
Adequate details	10 points
Creativity	5 points
Followed directions	5 points
Mechanics	5 points
Neatness	5 points
	50 points

Steps:

❶ Fold your paper in half like a book. Then, fold two inches back at each end to create two inside flaps.

❷ Design a cover for the book. It should include a picture, a title, and the author's name.

❸ On the inside front flap, write a summary of the book.

❹ On the inside back flap, write a short biography of the author.

❺ On the back cover, write a review of the book.

Feelings Accordion Book

What you'll need:

a large sheet of construction paper, colored pencils or markers, lined white paper

Steps:

1 Choose a character from your book.

2 Fold the construction paper in half the long way. Cut it along the fold.

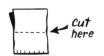 ← Cut here

3 Tape the two halves together along the short ends creating one long sheet.

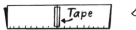 Tape

4 Make an accordion book by folding the paper to the right about one-third of the way. Then, take that third and fold it back one-third of the way. Continue folding until you have reached the end. You should have six sections on each side of your paper.

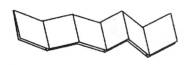

5 Find ten sentences in your story that express the feelings of the character.

6 Write each feeling sentence on a sheet of lined paper.

7 On the first section of your accordion book, write the title and author of your biography. Then add an illustration related to some aspect of your book.

8 On the remaining pages, write your sentences in a logical order. Draw and color an illustration to go with each of the ten sentences.

9 When you run out of room on the front, turn your paper over.

10 For the last section of the accordion book, choose one of the feelings that you've also experienced. Write the feeling at the top of the section and tell about the time you had this feeling. If you have room, draw a picture.

Grading Criteria	
Ten sentences	15 points
Illustrations	15 points
Organization	10 points
Followed directions	5 points
Neat/colorful	5 points
	50 points

Book Talk

Steps:

❶ Write the following about your book on a sheet of lined paper:

✳ Title and author

✳ A brief retelling of the story. Make sure you include the main events from the beginning, middle, and end of the book.

✳ A description of your favorite part of the book.

❷ Using your paper, give an oral presentation on your book to the rest of the class.

Grading Criteria

Written retelling	20 points
Oral retelling	20 points
Followed directions	5 points
Mechanics	5 points
	50 points

Children's Book

What you'll need:

white construction paper, colored pencils or markers, stapler

Steps:

❶ Create a children's book about your biography subject that would appeal to young children.

❷ Begin by writing a summary of your book. Then, simplify the summary, using language a young child would understand.

❸ Decide what information you will include on each page of your book. Your book should have a title page and at least ten pages of information.

❹ Create illustrations to go with the text.

❺ Design a cover for your book. It should include a title, your name, and a colorful illustration.

Grading Criteria

Information	20 points
Presentation/layout	15 points
Illustrations	10 points
Neat/colorful	5 points
	50 points

Biography

Memory Box

What you'll need:

shoe box, paper for decorating the shoe box, colored pencils or markers, various objects (see below)

Grading Criteria	
Written explanation	20 points
Oral retelling	15 points
Objects' relationship to biography	5 points
Followed directions	5 points
Mechanics	5 points
	50 points

Steps:

❶ Think of at least five objects that will help you retell the life story of the subject of your biography. The items will need to fit in a shoe box.

❷ Write an explanation of each object. Explain how the object relates to the person's life story.

❸ Decorate the outside of the shoe box so it reflects the content of the biography.

❹ Present your objects and your explanations to the class.

Design a CD Cover

What you'll need:

two 3-inch squares of white paper, colored pencils or markers, empty CD case (optional)

Grading Criteria	
Information (song titles)	20 points
Presentation/layout	15 points
Illustrations	10 points
Neat/colorful	5 points
	50 points

Steps:

❶ On one square of paper, create a cover for a CD that is related to your book. Decide on a title for the CD that incorporates your biography subject's name. Include an illustration of the person doing something. Color your cover.

❷ On the other square, make up ten song titles that include facts about the biography subject. Make an illustration for the back cover that relates to one of the song titles.

❸ If possible, display your CD cover in an empty case.

Biography Map

What you'll need:

9-by-18-inch sheet of white construction paper, colored pencils or markers

Steps:

❶ Design your own biography map. Be sure it includes the following:

✳ nine important life events

✳ physical description of the main subject

✳ most memorable event in the person's life

✳ examples of hardship faced in life

✳ information about the person's birth or death

✳ one brave moment

Grading Criteria

Biography map design	5 points
Life-event identification	5 points
Physical description	5 points
Memorable moment	5 points
Hardship	5 points
Birth/death	5 points
Brave moment	5 points
Followed directions	5 points
Mechanics	5 points
Neat/colorful	5 points
	50 points

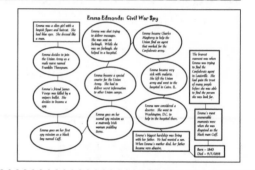

Write a Letter

Steps:

❶ Write a friendly letter to your biography subject.

❷ In your letter, include questions you would like to have answered that were not answered in the book.

❸ Your letter must be at least three-quarters of a page, typed.

Grading Criteria

Written letter	25 points
Organization	15 points
Mechanics	5 points
Neatness	5 points
	50 points

Personal Development Chart ———————————— Biography

Name _____ Date _____

Book Title: _____

Author: _____

As you read your novel, fill in the boxes below.

Person's Name: _____

Personal Description	Initial Feelings About Person—Chapters 1 & 2

Personal Development—Chapters ___ to ___	Personal Development—Chapters ___ to ___

Ending Description of the Person	How Did the Person Change?

Person's Toughest Obstacle	Person's Growth Rating (Circle a Number)
	1 **2** **3** **4** **5** low high On the back of this sheet, tell why you rated your character this way.

Grading Summary ———————————— Biography

	Possible Score	My Score

☐ **Personal Development Chart**

	Possible Score	My Score
Personal-life details	20 points	_____
Personal descriptions	10 points	_____
Rating	5 points	_____
Followed directions	5 points	_____
Mechanics	5 points	_____
Neatness	5 points	_____
	50 points	_____

☐ **Book Jacket**

	Possible Score	My Score
Organization	10 points	_____
Illustrations	10 points	_____
Adequate details	10 points	_____
Creativity	5 points	_____
Followed directions	5 points	_____
Mechanics	5 points	_____
Neatness	5 points	_____
	50 points	_____

☐ **Feelings Accordion Book**

	Possible Score	My Score
Ten sentences	15 points	_____
Illustrations	15 points	_____
Orgainization	10 points	_____
Followed directions	5 points	_____
Neat/colorful	5 points	_____
	50 points	_____

☐ **Book Talk**

	Possible Score	My Score
Written retelling	20 points	_____
Oral retelling	20 points	_____
Followed directions	5 points	_____
Mechanics	5 points	_____
	50 points	_____

☐ **Children's Book**

	Possible Score	My Score
Information	20 points	_____
Presentation/layout	15 points	_____
Illustrations	10 points	_____
Neat/colorful	5 points	_____
	50 points	_____

Grading Summary ———————————————— Biography

	Possible Score	**My Score**

❏ Memory Box ....

	Possible Score	My Score
Written explanation	20 points	_____
Oral retelling	15 points	_____
Objects' relationship to biography	5 points	_____
Followed directions	5 points	_____
Mechanics	5 points	_____
	50 points	_____

❏ Design a CD Cover ....

	Possible Score	My Score
Information (songs)	20 points	_____
Presentation/layout	15 points	_____
Illustrations	10 points	_____
Neat/colorful	5 points	_____
	50 points	_____

❏ Biography Map ....

	Possible Score	My Score
Biography map design	5 points	_____
Life-event identification	5 points	_____
Physical description	5 points	_____
Memorable moment	5 points	_____
Hardship	5 points	_____
Birth/death	5 points	_____
Brave moment	5 points	_____
Followed directions	5 points	_____
Mechanics	5 points	_____
Neat/colorful	5 points	_____
	50 points	_____

❏ Write a Letter ....

	Possible Score	My Score
Written letter	25 points	_____
Organization	15 points	_____
Mechanics	5 points	_____
Neatness	5 points	_____
	50 points	_____

Total for all three projects _____

Science Fiction Projects

Name _____ Due Date _____

Book Title:_____

✦ Make a tic-tac-toe by choosing three projects to complete for your novel.

Science Fiction News	**Cause and Effect Chart**	**Five Events**
Author Poster	**Character Web**	**Comic Strip**
Journal Entries	**Character Connections**	**Understanding Setting**

Science Fiction News

— Science Fiction

What you'll need:

9-by-18-inch sheet of white construction paper, colored pencils or markers

Grading Criteria	
Headline story	10 points
Weather report	10 points
Ads	10 points
Sports story	10 points
Appropriate graphics	5 points
Movie description	5 points
	50 points

Steps:

❶ Fold the construction paper in half like a book.

❷ Use the paper to design a newspaper based on your book. Use all blank sides of the folded sheet. Include the following items in your newspaper:

✳ newspaper name

✳ headline story

✳ weather report

✳ three to five ads

✳ five to eight pictures

✳ sports story

✳ movie description: Describe a movie that could be made in the setting of your book.

❸ Decide how to lay out the items. Remember, newspapers do not have any open space. Be creative!

 Collecting Team News

Unknown Planet - Three members of a collecting team lost three years ago have been found and are on their way back to earth tonight. The three crew members Gus Peters, Clyde Holdreth, and Lee Davidson were found when another collecting team, Colleting Team 504, landed on this unknown planet to complete a routine investigation of the habitat. The crew members from Collecting Team 504 stated that the crew members attacked the ship and were a little disoriented. They made the crew of team 504 take off as soon as Gus, Clyde and Lee were on board. Gus, Clyde and Lee told an incredible story of how their ship's drive was wreaked repeated and they were unable to take off from the planet. They three missing crew members were living in a house waiting for someone to rescue them. The three are resting comfortably in a local hospital. They should be able to return home in a few months after they have been debriefed.

Weather

Mon.	Strong Winds	Hi 69 F	L 39 F
Tues.	Cloudy	Hi 53 F	L 42 F
Wed.	AM Showers	Hi 62 F	L 38 F
Thurs.	Showers	Hi 59 F	L 39 F
Fri.	Mostly Cloudy	Hi 58 F	L 38 F
Sat.	Cloudy	Hi 60 F	L 37 F
Sun.	Sunny	Hi 65 F	L 43 F

Index

Top Story	Page 1
Weather Report	Page 1
Ads	Page 3
Sports	Page 2
Movie Description	Page 2

Current Surface

Science Fiction

Cause and Effect Chart

Grading Criteria

Cause retelling	15 points
Event retelling	15 points
Paragraph	10 points
Mechanics	5 points
Followed directions	5 points
	50 points

What you'll need:

two copies of the Cause and Effect sheet (page 96), 9-by-18-inch sheet of white construction paper, glue

Steps:

1 Complete two Cause and Effect sheets for your book. (Remember that the cause is the reason that an event happens. The effect is what happens. To find the cause, ask yourself, "Why did it happen?" To find an effect, ask yourself, "What happened?")

2 On the arrows, write a cause or action. In the box, write the result of this action.

3 Once you have all four pairs completed, cut out the arrows and the boxes.

4 Glue them on the construction paper vertically in the order they happened.

5 On a separate sheet of paper, write a paragraph telling which pair was the most important to the story and why you feel this way.

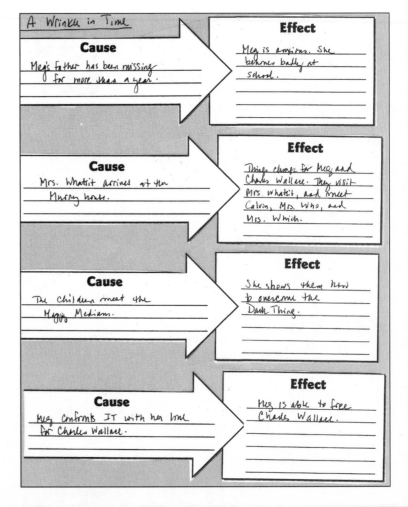

A Wrinkle in Time

Cause
Meg's father has been missing for more than a year.

Effect
Meg is anxious. She behaves badly at school.

Cause
Mrs. Whatsit arrives at the Murry house.

Effect
Things change for Meg and Charles Wallace. They visit Mrs. Whatsit, and meet Calvin, Mrs. Who, and Mrs. Which.

Cause
The children meet the Happy Medium.

Effect
She shows them how to overcome the Dark Thing.

Cause
Meg confronts IT with her love for Charles Wallace.

Effect
Meg is able to free Charles Wallace.

Five Events

Science Fiction

What you'll need:

Five Events sheet (page 97)

Grading Criteria

Five-events retellings	15 points
Paragraph	15 points
Ranked order	5 points
Followed directions	5 points
Mechanics	5 points
Neatness	5 points
	50 points

Steps:

❶ Complete the Five Events sheet by listing the five most important events from the book you read.

❷ Rank these events from 1 to 5, 1 being the most important event and 5 being the least important.

❸ Write a paragraph telling why you ranked the events in this order.

Five Events ——————— Science Fiction

Name _Elana_   Date _Dec. 13_

List five important events from your story. Rank these events in order of importance, with 1 being the most important and 5 the least. On the back of this sheet, write a paragraph explaining your ranking.

1. The ship's drive is wrecked.

2. The team is forced to land on a planet.

3. The repaired drive is damaged one night.

4. The team rations food.

5. The team learns to work together.

Author Poster

What you'll need:

9-by-18-inch sheet of white construction paper, colored pencils or markers

Grading Criteria	
Author biography	20 points
Author illustration	15 points
Followed directions	5 points
Adequate details	5 points
Neatness	5 points
	50 points

Steps:

❶ On the construction paper, draw and color a picture of the author of your biography.

❷ Write a short biography of the author. Be sure to include the following information:

　✳ Date of birth/death

　✳ Titles of other works

　✳ Where the author lives/lived

　✳ What the author likes/liked to do

　✳ Facts about the author's family

　✳ Any other interesting facts about the author

Character Web

What you'll need:

9-by-18-inch sheet of white construction paper, colored pencils or markers

Grading Criteria

Character selection	15 points
Topic statements	20 points
Followed directions	5 points
Adequate details	5 points
Neatness	5 points
	50 points

Steps:

❶ Draw a circle in the center of the construction paper. In the circle, draw a picture of an unusual character from your book. Make sure you include the character's name.

❷ Draw five large circles around the center circle. Label each circle as follows: "Appearance," "Actions," "Words," "Feelings," "Connection to Me." Then write a statement about the character that relates to each topic.

❸ Include somewhere on your map the title and author of your book.

Comic Strip

What you'll need:

9-by-18-inch sheet of white construction paper, colored pencils or markers

Steps:

❶ Fold the construction paper in half the long way. Fold it in half again like a book. Fold each of the ends in toward the center, stopping at the half fold. When you are finished folding, you should have eight squares.

❷ In the first box, write the name of the Comic Strip.

❸ In the remaining boxes, retell the plot of your book in comic-strip form. Create illustrations and dialogue boxes, and include speech balloons. Be sure your comic strip follows a logical sequence.

Grading Criteria

Illustrations	15 points
Dialogue	15 points
Creativity	10 points
Logical sequence	10 points
	50 points

Journal Entries

Science Fiction

What you'll need:

stapler, colored pencils or markers

Grading Criteria

Adequate details	20 points
Creativity	15 points
Followed directions	5 points
Mechanics	5 points
Neatness	5 points
	50 points

Steps:

1 Create a journal by folding five sheets of unlined white paper in half horizontally. Staple the journal together along the fold.

2 On the cover of the journal, write the book's title and the author's name.

3 Write journal entries, one per page, in response to the following prompts:

✱ Describe one character. Include a physical description, behaviors, and personality traits. Draw an illustration of the character.

✱ Make a list of ten unknown, interesting words and their definitions.

✱ Imagine yourself in a situation similar to one that a character is experiencing. Describe the character's situation. How did the character handle the situation? If you were in a similar situation, what would you do?

✱ Describe the main setting. Use examples from the story in your description. Do you know any place that would be similar to the story setting?

✱ Tell how you are the same as and different from one of the characters. Use examples from the story and from your own life.

✱ Write a letter telling the main character how you felt about what happened in the story. Make sure you include any questions you have about the story.

✱ Make two lists. One list should include all the good things that happened in the story, and the other list should include all the bad things that happened.

✱ Choose a quote from the story that you can relate to something in your life, a movie, or another book. Write the quote and explain why you chose it.

✱ Retell the ending of the story. Give your opinion of the ending.

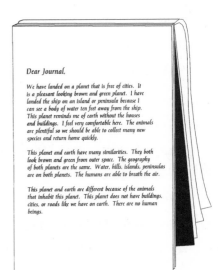

Dear Journal,

We have landed on a planet that is free of cities. It is a pleasant looking brown and green planet. I have landed the ship on an island or peninsula because I can see a body of water ten feet away from the ship. This planet reminds me of earth without the houses and buildings. I feel very comfortable here. The animals are plentiful so we should be able to collect many new species and return home quickly.

This planet and earth have many similarities. They both look brown and green from outer space. The geography of both planets are the same. Water, hills, islands, peninsulas are on both planets. The humans are able to breath the air.

This planet and earth are different because of the animals that inhabit this planet. This planet does not have buildings, cities, or roads like we have on earth. There are no human beings.

Science Fiction

Character Connections

What you'll need:

Character Connections sheet (page 98)

Steps:

❶ Choose two characters from your story. Put their names in the middle of the two webs on the Character Connection sheet. Find four words that describe each character and write those words in the boxes above and below the center ovals.

❷ In the boxes at the bottom, explain how the two characters are the same and how they are different.

❸ Decide which of the two characters you feel the strongest connection to. On the back of the sheet, explain what you have in common with this character.

Grading Criteria

Character descriptions	15 points
Character comparison	20 points
Followed directions	5 points
Mechanics	5 points
Neatness	5 points
	50 points

Understanding Setting

Steps:

❶ Write a paragraph describing the setting of your book. Be sure to include answers to the following questions in your paragraph:

✳ Where does the story take place?

✳ Does the setting seem real?

✳ When does the story take place? (time)

✳ What is the mood of the setting? (example: gloomy, frightening, tense, scary, happy)

❷ Write a second paragraph, explaining why you think the author chose to use this setting.

❸ Describe another time or place in which this story could have taken place. Use the answers to the questions above to describe your new setting.

Grading Criteria

Setting descriptions	15 points
Explanation	15 points
New setting	10 points
Mechanics	5 points
Neatness	5 points
	50 points

Cause and Effect ———— Science Fiction

Name _____ Date _____

Book Title: _____

Author: _____

Cause

Effect

Cause

Effect

Name _____ Date _____

List five important events from your story. Rank these events in order of importance, with 1 being the most important and 5 the least. On the back of this sheet, write a paragraph explaining your ranking.

Name _____ Date _____

Book Title: _____

Author: _____

Select two characters to compare. Put the name of each character into the center ovals of the webs. Write words that describe the two characters in the boxes.

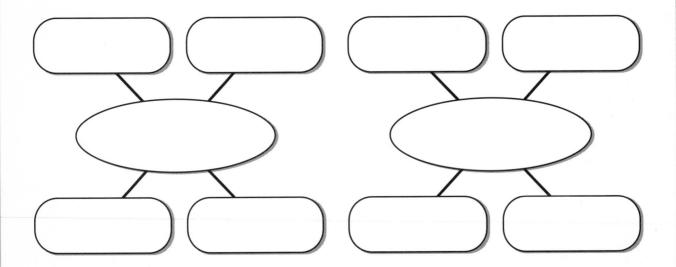

Tell how the two characters are the same and different.

Same	**Different**

On the back of this sheet, tell which character you feel the most connected to, and explain why.

Grading Summary ———————— Science Fiction

	Possible Score	My Score

☐ Science Fiction News ....

Headline story	.10 points	_____
Weather report	.10 points	_____
Ads	.10 points	_____
Sports story	.10 points	_____
Appropriate graphics	.5 points	_____
Movie description	.5 points	_____
	50 points	_____

☐ Cause and Effect Chart ....

Cause retelling	.15 points	_____
Event retelling	.15 points	_____
Paragraph	.10 points	_____
Mechanics	.5 points	_____
Followed directions	.5 points	_____
	50 points	_____

☐ Five Events ....

Five events retelling	.15 points	_____
Paragraph	.15 points	_____
Ranked order	.5 points	_____
Followed directions	.5 points	_____
Mechanics	.5 points	_____
Neatness	.5 points	_____
	50 points	_____

☐ Author Poster ....

Author biography	.20 points	_____
Author illustration	.15 points	_____
Followed directions	.5 points	_____
Adequate details	.5 points	_____
Neatness	.5 points	_____
	50 points	_____

☐ Character Web...

Character selection	.15 points	_____
Topic statements	.20 points	_____
Followed directions	.5 points	_____
Adequate details	5 points	_____
Neatness	.5 points	_____
	50 points	_____

Grading Summary ———————— Science Fiction

	Possible Score	My Score
☐ **Comic Strip**		
Illustrations . . . . .15 points		_____
Dialogue . . . . .15 points		_____
Creativity . . . . .10 points		_____
Logical sequence . . . . .10 points		_____
50 points		_____
☐ **Journal Entries**		
Adequate details . . . . .20 points		_____
Creativity . . . . .15 points		_____
Followed directions .5 points		_____
Mechanics . . . . .5 points		_____
Neatness . . . . 5 points		_____
50 points		_____
☐ **Character Connections**...................................		
Character descriptions . . . . .15 points		_____
Character comparison . . . . .20 points		_____
Followed directions .5 points		_____
Mechanics . . . . 5 points		_____
Neatness . . . . .5 points		_____
50 points		_____
☐ **Understanding Setting**		
Setting descriptions . . . . .15 points		_____
Explanation . . . . .15 points		_____
New setting . . . . .10 points		_____
Mechanics . . . . .5 points		_____
Neatness . . . . 5 points		_____
50 points		_____

Total for all three projects _____

Nonfiction Projects

Name _____ Due Date _____

Book Title:_____

✦ Make a tic-tac-toe by choosing three projects to complete for your novel.

Topic Report	**Fact Poster**	**Design an Ad**
Accordion Fact Book	**Vocabulary Dictionary**	**Book Review**
Newscast	**Pamphlet**	**Pop-Up Display**

Topic Report

Steps:

❶ Select an important topic or concept from your book.

❷ Research the topic or concept using the Internet or the library.

❸ Write a one-page report that gives information about the concept.

❹ Present the information you learned in an oral report to the class.

Grading Criteria	
Written report	20 points
Oral report	20 points
Followed directions	5 points
Mechanics	5 points
	50 points

Fact Poster

What you'll need:

a large sheet of construction paper, lined paper, pencil, colored pencils or markers

Steps:

❶ Choose ten fascinating facts from your book.

❷ On the construction paper, draw and color an illustration that relates to the subject of your book.

❸ Write the ten fascinating facts around the illustration.

❹ On a separate sheet of paper, write a paragraph telling why you chose these ten facts.

❺ Present your poster to the class.

Grading Criteria	
Ten facts	10 points
Presentation	10 points
Illustration	10 points
Written explanation	10 points
Followed directions	5 points
Mechanics	5 points
	50 points

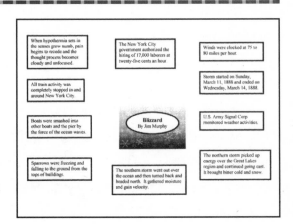

Design an Ad

What you'll need:

poster board, colored pencils or markers

Grading Criteria

Propaganda technique	15 points
Catchy slogan	10 points
Illustrations	10 points
Colorful	5 points
Followed directions	5 points
Neatness	5 points
	50 points

Steps:

❶ Design an ad to sell an item related to your nonfiction book. Begin by selecting a target audience and deciding which of the propaganda techniques described below you want to use to create your slogan.

❷ Use the answers to the following questions to help you design the ad:
  ✳ What are the benefits of this item?
  ✳ Why would everyone want to have it?
  ✳ How would you describe the item?

❸ Be sure your ad includes a strong visual image to communicate what you are selling.

Propaganda Techniques:

Generalization – Uses broad statements that mean little but create positive feelings.

Snob appeal – Suggests that people will be better than everyone else if they buy a product.

Testimonial – Has a well-known person voice his or her support of a product.

Bandwagon – Tries to convince people to buy something because everyone else is.

Repetition – Repeats a slogan over and over.

Half-truth – Uses facts and figures that favor one point of view while leaving out the facts and figures that support other viewpoints.

Name-calling – Criticizes a competing product.

Ordinary people – Tries to influence consumers by showing them that a product is liked by people "just like them."

Science appeal – Presents a scientific judgment that is not necessarily supported by facts.

Visit
Snow Shovel John
At
E. Ridley & Sons
Department Store

The only snow shovels available in town.

3000 Snow Shovels Available

Sturdy, metal shovels with strong handles

Help dig out the city by clearing away the snowdrifts in front of your building.

Accordion Fact Book

Nonfiction

What you'll need:

9-by-18-inch sheet of white construction paper, colored pencils or markers, tape

Steps:

1 Choose a character from your book.

2 Fold the construction paper in half the long way. Cut it along the fold.

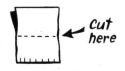

3 Tape the two halves together along the short ends creating one long sheet.

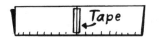

4 Make an accordion book by folding the paper to the right about one-sixth of the way. Then, take that sixth and fold it back one-sixth of the way. Continue folding until you have reached the end. You should have six sections on each side of your paper.

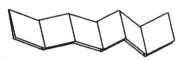

5 Find ten important facts in your nonfiction book. Write the facts on a sheet of lined paper.

6 On the first section, write the title and author of your book. Then add an illustration related to some aspect of your book.

7 On the remaining pages, write each of your facts. Create an illustration to go with each of the facts.

8 When you run out of room on the front, turn your paper over.

9 For the last section of the accordion book, write a conclusion about the facts you've collected. If you have room, draw a picture.

Grading Criteria	
Ten facts	35 points
Followed directions	5 points
Mechanics	5 points
Neat/colorful	5 points
	50 points

Vocabulary Dictionary

—Nonfiction

What you'll need:

white construction paper, colored pencils or markers

Steps:

❶ Make a dictionary of terms about your subject that could be used by younger students.

❷ Start by designing a cover for your dictionary using the construction paper. It should include an illustration of the subject matter and the title of your book. Make it colorful.

❸ Your dictionary must have at least twenty-five terms. For each term include the following items:

✳ the word

✳ an illustration

✳ a simple definition

✳ a sentence using the word

❹ Since you are creating a dictionary, the terms must be in alphabetical order.

❺ Your entries should be written neatly or typed.

Grading Criteria

25 subject terms	10 points
Definitions	10 points
Illustrations	10 points
Sentences	10 points
Alphabetical order	5 points
Cover design	5 points
	50 points

Blizzard Dictionary

Blizzard by Jim Murphy

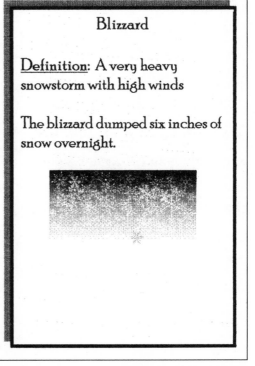

Blizzard

Definition: A very heavy snowstorm with high winds

The blizzard dumped six inches of snow overnight.

Book Review

Steps:

❶ Start your book review by creating a catchy title for it.

❷ Your book review should be at least half a page long. Don't summarize the entire book. Instead, pick the ideas you think would make someone else want to read the book. Tell just enough about the book to interest your audience.

❸ Use appealing vocabulary.

❹ Tell who you think should read the book.

❺ Share your book review with the class.

Grading Criteria

Written book review	15 points
Oral presentation	10 points
Catchy title	5 points
Interesting vocabulary	5 points
Followed directions	5 points
Mechanics	5 points
Neatness	5 points
	50 points

Newscast

Steps:

❶ Write a summary of your book.

❷ Rewrite your summary as if it were a special report from a TV station. (You may want to listen to a few newscasts so you understand how news reports sound.) Your summary should be no longer than 2 minutes.

❸ Present your news story to the class. Remember to:

✳ introduce yourself as the reporter.

✳ maintain eye contact with your audience. (Practice before the presentation day so you don't have to keep looking at your notes.)

✳ give the topic of your report.

✳ deliver the summary of the book.

❹ All of this should only take two minutes. The idea is to present as much information as possible in a short amount of time.

Grading Criteria

Summary	15 points
Two-minute time limit	10 points
Report language	10 points
Eye contact	5 points
Followed directions	10 points
	50 points

Pamphlet

What you'll need:

small sheet of white construction paper, colored pencils or markers, ruler

Grading Criteria

Layout of pamphlet	10 points
Catchy title	5 points
Summary	5 points
Points of interest	5 points
Contact information	5 points
Other books	5 points
Followed directions	5 points
Mechanics	5 points
Neatness	5 points
	50 points

Steps:

❶ Create an informational pamphlet about the topic of your nonfiction book. Start by placing the construction paper in front of you horizontally. Fold the left one-third of the paper toward the middle. Fold the right one-third backward toward the middle to create a trifold pamphlet.

❷ On the front flap of your pamphlet, write a catchy title and draw a colorful illustration.

❸ Open to the center sections.

Left section—List five exciting or interesting facts you learned.

Middle section—List others books in which more information can be found on the same subject.

Right section—List contact information, such as the following:

✳ your name

✳ a telephone number where you can be reached

✳ times when you are available to talk to individuals

✳ an explanation of why you are an expert on this subject

❹ Open your pamphlet to the back panels. On one panel, write a summary of the book. On the other panel, write a paragraph explaining who should read the book.

❺ Make sure your pamphlet is neat, colorful, and eye-catching.

How to Survive A Snowstorm

Pop-Up Display

Nonfiction

What you'll need:

9-by-12-inch pieces of oaktag, scissors, colored pencils or markers, ruler

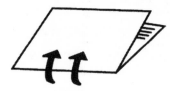

Steps:

❶ Fold the oaktag in half. Make a smooth, even crease.

❷ Use a ruler to draw the tabs on which you will glue each object that "pops up." The tabs should be at least one inch long, and about one-half inch wide.

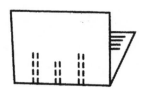

❸ Cut the tabs on the vertical lines only.

❹ Open the folded oaktag. Pull the tabs inside and crease the fold to make the background stand up.

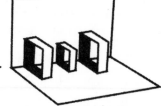

❺ Make pop-up pieces related to facts presented in your book. Glue the pieces onto the tabs.

❻ Color the background of the oak tag.

❼ Write a paragraph explaining your choices on lined paper.

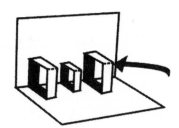

Grading Criteria	
Facts	10 points
Background design	10 points
Pop-up pictures	10 points
Book construction	10 points
Followed directions	5 points
Neat/colorful	5 points
	50 points

Grading Summary ———————————————— Nonfiction

	Possible Score	My Score

❏ Topic Report

Written report	.20 points	_____
Oral report	.20 points	_____
Followed directions	.5 points	_____
Mechanics	5 points	_____
	50 points	_____

❏ Fact Poster

Ten facts	.10 points	_____
Presentation	.10 points	_____
Illustration	.10 points	_____
Written explanation	.10 points	_____
Followed directions	5 points	_____
Mechanics	.5 points	_____
	50 points	_____

❏ Design an Ad

Propaganda technique	.15 points	_____
Catchy slogan	.10 points	_____
Illustrations	.10 points	_____
Colorful	.5 points	_____
Followed directions	5 points	_____
Neatness	.5 points	_____
	50 points	_____

❏ Accordion Fact Book

Ten facts	.35 points	_____
Followed directions	.5 points	_____
Mechanics	.5 points	_____
Neat/colorful	5 points	_____
	50 points	_____

❏ Vocabulary Dictionary

25 subject terms	.10 points	_____
Definitions	.10 points	_____
Illustrations	.10 points	_____
Sentences	.10 points	_____
Alphabetical order	.5 points	_____
Cover design	5 points	_____
	50 points	_____

Grading Summary ——————————— Nonfiction

	Possible Score	My Score

☐ Book Review ....

Written book review . . . . .15 points		_____
Oral presentation . . . . .10 points		_____
Catchy title . . . . .5 points		_____
Interesting vocabulary .5 points		_____
Followed directions . . . . 5 points		_____
Mechanics . . . . 5 points		_____
Neatness . . . . .5 points		_____
50 points		_____

☐ Newscast ....

Summary . . . . 15 points		_____
Two-minute time limit .10 points		_____
Report language . . . . .10 points		_____
Eye contact . . . . 5 points		_____
Followed directions . . . . .10 points		_____
50 points		_____

☐ Pamphlet ....

Layout of pamphlet . . . . .10 points		_____
Catchy title . . . . .5 points		_____
Summary . . . . .5 points		_____
Points of interest . . . . .5 points		_____
Contact information .5 points		_____
Other books . . . . .5 points		_____
Followed directions .5 points		_____
Mechanics . . . . .5 points		_____
Neatness . . . . 5 points		_____
50 points		_____

☐ Pop-Up Display ....

Facts . . . . .10 points		_____
Background design . . . . .10 points		_____
Pop-up pictures . . . . .10 points		_____
Book construction . . . . .10 points		_____
Followed directions .5 points		_____
Neat/colorful . . . . 5 points		_____
50 points		_____

Total for all three projects _____

Professional References

Cochran, Judith. *Everything You Need to Know to Be a Successful Whole Language Teacher*. Nashville, TN: Incentive Publications, 1993.

Garcia, Adela. *Learning Through Literature*. Cypress, CA: Creative Teaching Press, 1988.

Hiatt, Catherine. & Doug Wolven. *More Alternatives to Worksheets*. Cypress, CA: Creative Teaching Press, 1994.

Marriott, Donna. *What Are the Other Kids Doing?… While You Teach Small Groups*. Cypress, CA: Creative Teaching Press, 1997.

O'Brien-Palmer, Michelle. *Book-Talk*. Kirkland, WA: MicNik Publications, 1993.

O'Brien-Palmer, Michelle. *Read and Write*. Kirkland, WA: MicNik Publications, 1994.

Routman, Regie. *Conversations*. Portsmouth, NH: Heinemann, 2000.

Routman, Regie. *Invitations: Changing as Teachers and Learners K–12*. Portsmouth, NH: Heinemann, 1994.

Witmer, Laura. *Instant Independent Reading Response Activities*. New York, NY: Scholastic, 2001.

Wooten, Deborah A. *Valued Voices*. Newark, DE: International Reading Association, 2000.

Notes